Praise for
My Father Against the Nazis

"This beautifully written memoir, with its intimate storytelling and insightful historical reflection, is an urgent call for vigilance, compassion, and the courage to confront history head-on."
–Rabbi Andrue Kahn, Executive Director, The American Council for Judaism

"This book is a powerful reminder that fascism and hate are constant threats to every generation's humanity and peace."
–Henry A. J. Ramos, Author, *Democracy & The Next American Economy*

"A true tale of a family experiencing Nazi hatred and aggression told with expertise and compassion that serves as a reminder of how we can raise ourselves up in the face of tragedy."
–Marion Angelica, Artist

"Couldn't put it down."
–Ken Neil, Classmate

"What a tremendous piece of creativity and craftmanship. You are an inspiring, crystal-clear writer. Really impressed. Continued courage to you."
–Peter Faber, Film and Stage Actor

"It's a real gut punch but worth the pain. Well done."
–Steve Sherlock, Vietnam Veteran

"The author delivers this story with the attention of a mid-wife and the fierceness of a warrior."
–Ruth Dreier, Listener

"As a rabbi's son and musical chronicler of love and loss, this book speaks to my human, Jewish heart."
–Si Kahn, Founder, Bend the Arc: A Jewish Partnership for Justice

"It's just freaking incredible - in scope, heartbreak, depravity, cruelty, resilience - and especially your reminiscences."
—Jerry Croxdale, Athlete

"Emotionally exhausting in the very best way."
—Claudia Kittock, Teacher

"The stories of real people in real settings are hard to put down."
—Carla Tollefsrud, Reader

"Overall, A+"
—Michael Rothman, History Professor

"Those Newsreels add important lessons, so if you're a history buff, you've come to the right place."
—Vance Levesque, History Buff

My Father Against the Nazis

Minneapolis

SECOND EDITION NOVEMBER 2025
My Father Against the Nazis Copyright © 2025 by Steven E. Mayer.
All rights reserved.

No part of this book may be used or reproduced in any manner whatsoever without written permission except in the case of brief quotations used in critical articles and reviews.

For information, write to Calumet Editions,
6800 France Avenue South, Suite 370, Edina, MN 55435

10 9 8 7 6 5 4 3 2
ISBN: 978-1-962834-52-0

Interior and cover design: Gary Lindberg
Cover art by Jane Lake Birt

My Father Against the Nazis

Steven E. Mayer

CALUMET
EDITIONS
Minneapolis

Also by Steven E. Mayer

How to Save the World: Evaluating Your Choices

Published by Wisdom Editions, an imprint of Calumet Editions, October 2023. Available in print and digital form.
ISBN: 978-1-962834-00-1.

*Building Community Capacity:
The Potential of Community Foundations*

Published by Rainbow Research, Inc., 1994. Available as download from www.EffectiveCommunities.com.
ISBN: 0-9624428-4-4.

Either we have hope within us or we do not.

It is a dimension of the soul and is not essentially dependent on some particular observation of the world.

HOPE is an orientation of the spirit, an orientation of the heart. It transcends the world that is immediately experienced and is anchored somewhere beyond its horizons.

HOPE in this deep and powerful sense is not the same as joy that things are going well or willingness to invest in enterprises that are obviously headed for early success, but rather an ability to work for something because it is good, not because it stands a chance to succeed.

HOPE is definitely not the same thing as optimism. It is not the conviction that something will turn out well, but certainty that something makes sense regardless of how it turns out.

It is HOPE, above all which gives the strength to live and continually try new things.

— Vaclav Havel

Dedicated to my mother
Margaret Koch Mayer
who had occasion to say to me,
"I wish you knew Paul
the way he was when I met him."

Contents

Introduction 1
Book 1: Pre-War 11
Book 2: War... 89
Book 3: Post-War 153
Wrapping Up 205
Acknowledgements 215
About the Author 217

Author's Note

When I submitted the first draft of this book to the editor, I was an 80-year old with fire in my belly and a lifelong hurt in my heart. The title then was "*My Father Against the Fucking Nazis*," which pretty much made clear where I was coming from.

But the editor said, "This will never do. We can't have fucking in the title – the booksellers won't stand for it." Eventually, with the world outside looking more like another Nazi storm rising, they said maybe we could put it back in – but with an asterisk in the middle of the offending word. But if one can't say "fucking Nazis" with venom, why settle for a sly, possibly humorous work-around, I wondered. I said no thanks, but was given permission to use it in the text, sparingly.

As I continued to fuss with the entire draft, working on the editor's advice to move from tedious litany toward more enlivened and soulful text, an interesting thing happened: I got a lot deeper into the heart and mind of my father, and came to understand and appreciate the complexities of life so much more. I explain this and the current title in the last section, Wrapping Up.

Paul A. Mayer, 1935, near Köln. Photo by Margaret Koch. "One of my favorite pictures of your father when we were getting to know each other," she said.

Introduction

I'm in Amsterdam, sitting on the rooftop patio of my four-hundred-year-old canal house smoking a lovely, small Indonesian cigar I bought at *P.G.C. Hajenius*, Amsterdam's oldest and finest cigar and tobacco shop. From here, I can survey the rooftops and courtyard treetops of my neighboring canal houses, most of them built two hundred or more years ago.

I can see the bell tower of the old West Church off to the right and the old Amsterdam Central train station to the left. Every quarter of an hour those church bells mark the time and a train leaves in the direction of Germany. Those are both powerful reminders of why I'm here writing this book.

An old nickname for Amsterdam is "Mokum," meaning something like "safe harbor." It's an endearing name, and I'm frequently reminded of its protective essence. I've visited this beautiful city for years and know it well. My wife and partner Susan and I now live here much of the year, thanks to the German/European Union passport I secured many years ago to escape the impending right-wing storm rising in the United States, and to live in safety, a theme invoked often in this book.

***

In 1959 while in high school, we performed *The Diary of Anne Frank*. As the curtain rises, the West Church bells ring as my character Otto Frank, Anne's father, slowly surveys the room through the smoke-like haze, having just returned from the Auschwitz death camp as the sole family survivor. He spots Anne's dusty old book on the floor, painfully bends over to pick it up, and slowly opens it, as Anne's voice from the void supplies the opening lines from her diary.

For the occasion of acting in this play, my father allowed me to wear the old topcoat he had worn on the ship over from England with my mother just as World War II was turning hot twenty years earlier. It was made of cellulose, a new material made during the Depression when wool was scarce, which weighed a ton but was always stylish. He kept it in his closet alongside his US Army uniform.

In the audience were my parents and grandmother. My grandmother actually knew Otto. They were practically neighbors in Frankfurt in the early 1920s and were good friends before Otto met the woman who later became the mother of Anne Frank. They even went to each other's weddings.

Performing in front of my parents, and especially my grandmother, was surreal. She watched me play the role of Otto Frank, perhaps her suitor as family legend speculates. I was only sixteen years old, and only barely comprehended the real depth of this drama, but it has always felt like a Twilight Zone kind of moment.

We performed this only a few years after Anne's diary was first discovered in her Amsterdam annex, and only a few years after the play based on that diary was performed on Broadway. It created a sensation at the time. It was new in the consciousness of Americans and created a whole new avenue for understanding what happened during World War II.

Our production ran only two nights. It went well. "After all is said and done," Anne's voice intones as the stage lights finally dim. "In spite of everything, I still believe people really are good at heart," is Anne's last line in the play, and the line I most remember; it never fails to produce goosebumps.

***

My Father Against the Nazis

A few days after my performance, and still flush with the excitement of staging this moving play, I was emboldened to open a conversation over breakfast with the family, all seated together in the kitchen–my father, mother, grandmother, and my younger brother. I was essentially still an unaware, dreamy, adolescent kid with close to zero emotional intelligence, so I just leaped into it.

I addressed my father, a man I didn't particularly like, and I was foolish in my approach. I knew that my parents and my grandmother had just barely escaped Nazi Germany, leaving everything behind. I knew they had succeeded in making their way to New York just as the war in Europe was getting underway. I knew that my father joined the US Army to fight the Nazis and rescue his parents in Köln, the city of his birth. I knew that the story was awful, but I knew little more, as they never discussed their story. I wanted more, and I knew *The Diary of Anne Frank* provided an opening.

"Tell me," I said, "because I don't really understand. What exactly happened to your parents?"

My father slowly looked up from his soft-boiled egg and burst into tears, his mouth wide open but with no sound and no words. It was a silent scream of unspeakable pain from deep within, like in the famous painting by Edward Munch.

The Silent Scream, by Edward Munch, 1895

After a few moments of awkward silence, my mother spoke and provided the briefest answer. "After we fled Germany to England and then America, we learned that Paul's parents were rounded up from their home in Köln and taken to Theresienstadt, a concentration camp in Czechoslovakia. When the war was finally over, we learned that they survived Theresienstadt for over a year but then, six months after you were born, they were taken to Auschwitz, an extermination camp in Poland, where they were killed on arrival in one of those gas chambers."

***

As a child, and then growing into adolescence and beyond, the dominant memory I had of my father was of him hunched over a typewriter at his desk, wreathed in cigarette smoke, thinking hard between flurries of typing. I'd ask what he was doing, but he'd brush me away, "Not now, *Steviechen*," using the diminutive German form of family affection he used for me all his life.

I came to learn he was working on legal briefs to be used to sue the post-war government of Germany for restitution and compensation for all that the Nazi regime had stolen from him. He was suing for a restoration of his former life, the life that was meant for him and his family, violently stolen by the fucking Nazis who had taken over the country he had loved. Over time, he was successful in the technicalities of this restoration, but still miserable in the constant reminders of his losses.

***

"Here's the good stuff," my mother told me a few short years after my father's memorial service. "I've thrown out all the legal files, the court records, the endless back and forth with the lawyers. We're done with all that. But the real story is here. Maybe you'd like to do something with this, maybe write something…"

I had already written a few things about my father and my parents' travails growing up in the time of Hitler, their escape, and the anguish of their losses. One such paper, "*Mein Kampf, Part II*" is included as a section in this book. My father was hard to grow up with, and harder to write about. He was often sullen and withdrawn, and when he'd show up he was critical and judgmental. There'd be occasional humor or intelligence, which I enjoyed, and also occasional affection, which I didn't trust. They say that growing up in a grief-stricken home leaves many marks.

My mother's suggestion stayed with me, and I eventually took her up on it. I let the boxes sit for a while to let the memories marinate while I continued my career. Between teaching and consulting opportunities I sporadically found time to scan and inventory the contents and send packages of the originals to be archived at the Leo Baeck Institute in New York, an organization devoted to commemorating the German Jewish emigration experience. My parents had belonged since its earliest days and contributed to its archiving efforts.

First out of storage was a picture I'd known since childhood. It had always hung by my father's desk and had always intrigued me. It's a lithograph of a distinguished young man in rabbinic garb, captioned "Dr. S. Mayer, Rabbi in Hechingen." I looked it up and was astounded by what had become of his synagogue in southwest Germany since it was destroyed by Hitler's storm troopers in November 1938.

Dr. Samuel Mayer, Rabbi in Hechingen (Germany), ca. 1830,

It wasn't long before all Jews who refused to flee for their lives were hunted down, rounded up, and sent away.

Years later, in the 1980s, the synagogue was restored beautifully under the aegis of the Initiative Hechingen Synagoge, a *bona fide* foundation with a Board of Directors, educational programs and a meaningful budget. It's a historical monument. Amnesty International even had a presence there for a while in the 1980s when refugee Jews, this time from the Soviet Union, settled briefly there but then moved on.

***

"I'm Steven Mayer, son of Paul Mayer, grandson of Ernst Mayer, great grandson of Adolf Mayer, and great-great-grandson of Samuel Mayer," I wrote to the Synagoge Initiative by way of introduction. I heard back immediately. "It fills me with great joy that you have contacted us! I work as a research and teaching assistant for the Initiative Hechingen Synagoge, the association which owns the Old Synagogue. Dr. Samuel Mayer is a major historical figure in every tour of the synagogue I give. I have always wondered about his descendants. Up until your email, I knew only about Samuel Mayer's sons and some of their children, and that's all. Please visit."

This was an opportunity, and Susan and I jumped on it. My ancestors on both sides had been born in the Rhineland. My father was from Köln and my mother from Frankfurt, and their family for generations were from smaller towns in the region. We drove from Frankfurt up one side of the Rhineland and down the other, visiting these towns and countryside of my heritage. And the old Jewish cemeteries—oh, the cemeteries! Tended mindfully by their neighbors, locked at night and home to songbirds that serenade residents and visitors alike, the cemeteries are stalwart reminders of history.

Then we returned to my Amsterdam rooftop garret, inspired to write.

***

My Father Against the Nazis

I sometimes write in Amsterdam's wonderful old cafes. Early on in this project, I went to the Café Hulscher at the Hotel Port van Cleve, just behind the Palace at Dam Square, an old establishment. It's where Paul and Margo had breakfast one morning in February 1938 while in Amsterdam to see if it would serve as a place to launch their newly married life while dodging the constant legal harassment and deprivations well underway in Germany just up the Rhine River.

Writing in my "professional reporter's notebook" (that's what it says on the cover) and sipping a Four Roses whiskey, which I'd learned to drink at my father's knee, I mused, *What on Earth is Paul thinking? Here it is, early 1938, and a huge majority of German Jews had heeded the writing on the wall and fled. But for Paul it's still 'Do we stay in Germany, or do we go?' Really? Was that still a question in February 1938?* Hitler had become dictator five years earlier. He disbanded the Constitution of the Republic and issued laws that disbarred my father as the newly minted High Court lawyer, eliminating his imagined future and knocking *his* father off his well-developed pedestal of honorable service and reputation. All pathways of opportunity were blocked, and they were being told by everyone it's time to leave. Plus, he'd just married the just-right woman, a woman of beauty and distinction whom he loved and who was eager to start a family.

Where did his future lie? In Germany, which had closed all doors and decertified him as a citizen and a man of the future? Or in Amsterdam? Or, God forbid, all the way across the ocean in America? How could my father and mother still think that life in Germany was still possible? But they did.

***

So, I've written about my father and his fight against the Nazis, but the story is more than that. The story of Nazi Germany has been one of the most enduring stories in the decades since it was defeated. All those books, movies, video games, comics, and serialized TV shows. The story of Nazi Germany as a big powerful force that violently sucked the life out of almost all of Europe, like some kind of madness that went viral, is still the story of our time, even though the war ended 80 years ago. Maybe this war didn't actually end, just as World War I morphed into World War II which morphed into the Cold War which morphed into contemporary culture wars.

I really don't want to write about the similarities of America in early 2025 with Germany in early 1933. America isn't Germany, and 2025 isn't 1933. Events will certainly play out differently now in the US, in Europe, and everywhere else. While this may come as a surprise to many who know me, I too believe, just like the diarist Anne Frank, that people are good at heart, or at least people are born that way, and then life happens. My belief is a hopeful one, perhaps belied by the facts. Whether the human race can draw enough strength from the forces of good to prevail over the forces of evil is a real question. My hopeful belief is paired with a pessimist's point of view.

This back-and-forth of waves and ripples, large and small, of societal good and bad, isn't new, it's the entire historical record. There is something about the waves and ripples of history and the question of whether history repeats itself, or whether the lessons of history are ever learned. This book is full of observations on those questions. There are huge ocean-like forces at work at the geographical, cultural, political, economic, and spiritual levels that drive the story of my father and the Nazis and billions of other individuals playing their parts as drops in this ever-restless ocean. In such a memoir it's necessary to remember a life in flux in a world in flux.

But no matter how much the world changes, comparisons of then and now are inevitable. My parents' assessment of their chances of a bright future while sitting at the Café Hulscher came from a different time, ninety years ago, with their privileged, young lives in front of them. Their calculus then is different from ours now. And hindsight changes the view considerably. Comparisons of then and now may be inevitable, and they invite consideration, but making them is not my real intent.

***

A huge part of Paul's story is the context—growing up in Germany in the first half of the twentieth century, one of the most tumultuous and consequential fifty-year periods in Western Civilization. So much was happening! Accelerating arcs of themes were going on for generations, reaching disastrous climaxes—and are still. The world he experienced, coming of age during the first World War was in such paroxysms of change that everyone was affected, from the so-called top to the so-called bottom the world over. And for many this change was so traumatic that few survivors could talk about it. It was Paul's silent trauma, his pain and distancing in a new world he by no means had chosen, that I experienced.

A tragedy, says the filmmaker Joel Coen, is where the character sees everything that's going on while at the same time is helpless to change the arc of events. That's Paul. At one point after the war and after he was largely done with his legal restitution work, Paul took up his pen and wrote articles for the esteemed German American newspaper, *Aufbau* ("Reconstruction").

Paul signed these opinion pieces with a pen name, "Cassandrus," after the character from ancient Greek and Roman stories who was gifted by the knowledge of the truth and the ability to speak it but doomed to be never believed. That is certainly Paul, especially in his year in London just ahead of the assault by the Nazis on the West, and just ahead of his reluctant flight to America.

***

In writing this book, I borrowed a trick from John Dos Passos' marvelous trilogy of early twentieth century American history—*The 42nd Parallel, 1919,* and *The Big Money*. At the beginning of many of his chapters he provides a "Newsreel," styled like headlines from the early days of cinematic journalism. They are meant to provide the view of the day from ten to thirty thousand feet up to remind the reader of the "real" events of the time. Dos Passos then riffs on these headlines and creates little stories as told through "A Camera's Eye"—stories told more biographically, impressionistically, and personally.

The news items included in my Newsreels come from readily accessible Internet sources. Some of those events were far away from the Mayer family, but with the premise that everything is interconnected, they provide context for the more local historical family events I describe.

I begin the story in 1907 when Paul was born, seven years after his father Dr. Ernst Mayer opened his medical practice in Köln exactly when the twentieth century began.

Book 1: Pre-War

A good start in life

Newsreel (1900–1907)

1900–In October of 1900, Dr. Ernst Mayer, age twenty-six, father of the "hero" of this story and grandfather of this writer, opens his medical practice in the old city of Köln.

1901–Queen Victoria dies after a reign of nearly sixty-four years, and is succeeded by her son, Edward VII.

1902–Approximately one hundred and fifty thousand United Mine Workers strike in Pennsylvania for a wage increase and more suitable hours.

1903–King Alexander of Serbia and his wife are assassinated by conspirators.

1904–The British reach a strategic agreement with France which includes mutual military support in the event of war. Six years earlier, Germany begins to build up its navy to challenge the British Navy's long-standing global supremacy.

1905–In January, troops of Russian Czar Nicholas II fire upon peaceful demonstrators in St. Petersburg killing hundreds in the riots that followed in what comes to be known as Bloody Sunday.

1907–Paul Adolf Mayer is born to Dr. Ernst Mayer and Frau ELisbeth Mayer (née Teutsch), in Köln (September 4).

***

Paul was fortunate to be born into quite favorable circumstances, and he grew up with an awareness of his family's history as well as the values of the times.

As soon as he was old enough, his Papa took him out for walks about the city of Köln. Little Paul was a precocious little boy, and he asked questions.

"What's that?" Paul asked. His father replied, didactically, "That's the river, the mighty Rhine River, the longest in western Europe. It starts high up in the Swiss Alps and flows down by lots of several important cities in Germany, all the way past us here and then through Holland and out to the North Sea."

Map of Contemporary Europe. Credit: Alamy.com

"And that?" Paul asked, pointing to an extremely large church tower.

"That," said Ernst, "is our famous Cathedral, the Dom. They started building it in 1248 and finished it only a few years ago. Almost all Köln's churches are Roman Catholic, not Lutheran, as Köln is one of Germany's most Catholic cities, though not as much as Trier where I was born. You'll love the Karnival, or *Mardi Gras* as the French call it, one of the biggest in Europe.

"Papa, why do they call it Köln? Shouldn't it be Cologne?"

Papa snorted and said, "Well, Cologne is what the French, English, and even the Americans call it, and the Dutch call it Keulen. But if you look at all those names real close you can see the word "colony," which is what the Romans meant when they founded this place as a colonial outpost almost two thousand years ago in the year 85 after Jesus.

"And those things?" Paul asked.

Ernst told him, "Those are river boats, *Paulchen*, and they push barges full of important cargo from one river town to another.

"Cargo?" asked Paul.

"Yes, like coal from the Ruhr Valley just up that way," Ernst said, pointing north, "which is useful in factories that make things. They also carry chemicals, and oil, and stuff for turning grains into food, from all over the interior of Germany. Köln has become a very important city these days, and young families are moving from the countryside to work in the city."

"Is that good?" Paul was a curious boy indeed.

"Well, yes, mostly," said his Papa. "It's good for me, because young families have young children, and I'm a bone doctor and they come to my office to see me."

"Why? And what's a bone doctor?" asked Paul.

"A bone doctor is an easy way of saying an orthopedic physician. I studied orthopedic medicine at the universities of Würzburg and Munich. Those two universities were very important because that's where Dr. Roentgen discovered X-rays, a very significant discovery for the practice of medicine, because with X-rays you can look inside a person's body and see all the bones. You can see if children's bones are deformed after they're born, and you can see where adults' bones are broken when they get into accidents, or when they're shot on the battlefield. The whole field of radiology was started then, and I'm proud to tell you, *Paulchen*, that I was part of that."

"Is that why I see kids my age limping into your office at home, and when they come out they have something around their leg and when I see them again they walk much better?" asked Paul.

"You're very observant, *Paulchen*. That thing around their leg is called a cast. You may have met my assistant who makes them, and he can make splints out of leather as well, which help them keep their bones straight while they're healing. And there's another exciting thing going on. I was asked to help start a radiology department at the Severins Klösterchen Hospital nearby, perhaps the first in Prussia, with the newest kind of X-ray machines. We're able to treat kids there, but also grown-ups who get into accidents, like at work on the boats or trains, or even just crossing these busy streets. Accidents happen, and bones break. I like to think I'm being useful in this day and age."

Paul looked up at his Papa, very proud, and asked him, "Were you a good student, Papa?"

"Good enough," replied Papa. "Not as good as that Einstein kid who was a student at Würzburg at the same time I was. I tell you what, *Paulchen*, he's going to amount to something, even though he wasn't really interested in medicine. Something about atomic theory, he said, which also has its origins in those same physics labs.

"But the important thing," continued Papa, "is that I was even allowed to go to university at all. If I had gone to a Talmud Torah, like your grandfather Adolf (yes, the same Adolf as in your middle name), or Adolf's father Rabbi Samuel (yes, that's the one whose picture hangs in our hallway), I wouldn't have had the kind of education that allows me to do all this. By the time I was born things had changed enough so that Jews... You know what, *Paulchen*, let's save that talk for next time. Let's just say all my early years of schooling that allowed me to go to university, I went to a Catholic school in Trier where I was born…"

"Wait," said Paul. "We're Jews? And why in God's name were you born in Trier? Why not Jerusalem?"

Sighing deeply, Papa said, "Well, *Paulchen*, that's a long story, something we can save for later. For now, I can tell you there's been a Jewish community here for centuries, ever since we tagged along with the Romans in developing this region."

Ernst Mayer as medical student, late 1890s

***

A few years earlier, in 1906, Ernst married ELisbeth Fanny Teutsch (aka Lisbeth), daughter of Julius Teutsch and Emma Cahan.

By the time Paul was born in 1907, Ernst had a medical practice that was doing quite well. Köln too was doing quite well. It was situated perfectly for the commercial economy created by the Industrial Revolution, and was becoming a thriving city. Best of all, urbanization tends to create the stresses that underlie a thriving medical practice, especially orthopedics.

Many Jewish families of the time credit Napoleon Bonaparte, the emperor of France, for creating some of the conditions that put this Mayer family on stable ground. Whatever one can say about his dictatorial position and style, he was "good for the Jews," a litmus test for many throughout Christendom throughout the generations. His reputation, like Abraham Lincoln's, is as "the great emancipator" of European Jewry, because it was Napoleon who opened the Jewish ghettoes throughout Prussia and liberated both Jewish and non-Jewish lives to the flowering of Enlightenment ideals. Pronounced in shorthand these ideals were '*Liberté, Égalité, Fraternité.*' "Jews are human beings and entitled to all the rights of all human beings." Napoleon said, in a statement that was radical then but enforced by his own imperial decree.

This marked the beginning of more integrated or assimilated lives for many Jews, though this varied from place to place. But by the late nineteenth century Gentiles were getting accustomed to Jews in their midst. Even with this progress, there was always an awareness that Germany, or the world, is a fickle place. Conflict always arises, and good times come and go, as do bad times. Throughout, Paul's elders deeply believed that embracing Enlightenment values could extend the chances that the good prevails.

And as Papa surely explained to his *Paulchen*, the revolutionary ideals promoted by Napoleon and his Enlightenment values infused much of the new Liberal (or Reformed) Judaism that Paul's great-grandfather Rabbi Samuel Mayer promoted. He had been a leader in advancing German Liberal Judaism, both in the synagogue and in his rapidly changing community of Hechingen in southwest Germany. And while one can say that all rabbis are essentially lawyers, Rabbi Samuel went back to University to become a secular lawyer, the first rabbi in Germany to do so, and with those skills he had the ear of the Hohenzollern prince who lived atop the hill nearby. The prince was married to Napoleon's daughter, and together they helped to break down barriers and smoothed over conflict between Jews and Gentiles. Ever since, there's been increased understanding and tolerance both ways, Papa surely explained.

That Samuel Mayer picture has hung in a Mayer household ever since it was created in the 1830s, and that's why the Synagogue Hechingen Initiative has the social mission it does. It's also why Papa could tell his *Paulchen*, "Thanks to Napoleon and my grandfather Samuel, you have the same rights as anyone else."

A great war emerges on the horizon

Newsreel (1906–1913)

1906–H.M.S. Dreadnought is launched by Britain, marking the advent of a new class of big-gun battleships. The Germans follow suit and begin building similar battleships as an all-out arms race ensues between Germany and Britain.

1907–Second Hague Peace Conference of forty-six nations adopts ten conventions on rules of war.

1908–Austria-Hungary, backed by Germany, annexes Bosnia-Herzegovina. Neighboring Serbia, with the backing of Russia, voices its objection in support of the Serbian minority living in Bosnia.

1910–Germany surpasses Britain as the leading manufacturing nation in Europe. The United States remains the world leader, surpassing all the European manufacturing nations combined.

1911–First use of aircraft as offensive weapon occurs in Turkish Italian War. Italy defeats Turks and annexes Libya.

1912–The "unsinkable" ocean liner Titanic sinks on maiden voyage after colliding with an iceberg; over 1,500 drown. Balkan Wars begin, resulting from territorial disputes. Woodrow Wilson is elected US president.

1913–London peace treaty partitions most of European Turkey among the victors of first Balkan War.

As an old saying goes, "the King giveth, and the King taketh away." While 1900 was a good time to begin a medical practice, success wasn't assured.

The time of Paul's early childhood saw increased prosperity in his homeland, but also volatility. Progress with the still-young Industrial Revolution wasn't entirely peaceful or smooth. In Köln and elsewhere in Europe, the forces of social upheaval and instability were rumbling right under Dr. Ernst Mayer's feet. Kingdoms and empires were increasing military production, clearly evident in Köln with its steel mills nearby. The economic and political world was heating up and had been for a while.

Riots rooted in class inequities flared up in Köln and elsewhere in the German Empire and throughout western Europe, most menacingly (or promisingly) in Russia. Powerful social forces challenged an orderly process of German evolution and pushed its trajectory this way and that. Already the German Empire was gearing up for war, a big war, the Great War that became known later as World War I. These developments defined almost the entirety of life in Germany in those years, and Paul was an impressionable youngster throughout.

Prussia, which included Köln at this time, was in the ascendancy, and the most influential state in the German Empire. Among the wealthy, fashion and elegance prevailed. The crowned heads of Europe, along with their retinues, spent time in fashionable resort towns like Baden-Baden. They frolicked and gambled in casinos and flaunted their wealth.

As Amos Elan wrote, "Germany was economically and militarily the most powerful nation on the European continent, although war was increasingly considered unlikely, if only because of its exorbitant cost."

"Bourgeois life was firmly grounded in the rule of law. In *The World of Yesterday*, written after Hitler's rise to power, Stefan Zweig looked back at the 'Golden Age of Security' half a century earlier, and wrote, 'Everything seemed based on permanency and the state itself was the chief guarantor of this stability. Whoever built a house looked upon it as a secure domicile for his children, grandchildren, and great-grandchildren.'"[1]

This was clearly the thinking of Paul's childhood home and family—the rule of law and a sense of stability guaranteed by the state.

But a big fight was brewing among the nations of Europe. Within Germany, pride in Germany as a great nation ran high. This period was the pinnacle of European nationalism and colonialism, but not yet of fascism. Germany and every other nation needed ever-more resources, materials, and cheap labor to keep their rising standards of living ever-rising. The upcoming, so-called Great War was the last among the mighty monarchs who'd been carefully married off for generations to form strategic alliances useful for only one thing: control of increasingly vast kingdoms and resources. Their governments had grown large and bloated with bureaucracies to manage the complexities of rapid growth and defend their interests. The Em-

---

[1] Amos Elon, *The Pity of It All: A Portrait of Jews in Germany 1743-1933*. Penguin Books, 2004

pires of Germany, Russia, and Great Britain were headed by first cousins who liked each other well enough but who otherwise felt compelled to settle their differences by fighting amongst themselves with armed forces.

These emperors could see the train wreck ahead but were unwilling to untangle their alliances of national interests, written and signed, figuratively at least, with their families' blood. Also showing up for the fight was the mighty Austro-Hungarian Empire, "Big Hungary" joined at the hip with "Big Austria." And together they were lashed to the long-powerful but now dying really big bull elephant, the Ottoman or Turkish Empire.

Each of those nations and tribes had been beaten before, and they each had been victorious before. They'd been at it for centuries in one configuration of alliances or another. No war settled anything for long. They were grieving and angry, with scores to settle. With every victory, the map changed, and who's in power changed, but the struggle was at heart the same.

Big riches were at stake. What were they fighting over? Gold. Land. Diamonds. Dominance. Markets. Cheap labor. The lives of millions and the treasures of centuries. Official slavery was over, but cheap labor was still needed to plant valuable crops on appropriated land and to extract mineral wealth from the ground. Nationalism, colonialism, and imperialism were all in play, as was "honor."

Was this a new thing, a product of the Industrial Age? Yes. Or was it an old thing, a continuation of the Old and New Testaments? Yes. There was no visible end to this conflict rooted in the demands of the Industrial Revolution with its incessant need for global growth. One can see it all clearly unfolding since the thirteenth century, as told in *A Distant Mirror*, by Barbara Tuchman.

***

In the midst of this escalation of tension, Ernst and Lisbeth have their second child, born in 1912, named Ilse but known to friends and family as "Illa." In more intimate family settings, she is forever referred to as *Das goldige Kind* ("the Golden Child").

Paul and Illa, ca. 1914

Newsreel (1914)

July 28—Austria declares war on Serbia as a direct result of the assassination of Archduke Francis Ferdinand at Sarajevo on June 28.

July 29—Russia begins general mobilization.

July 31—Germany begins mobilization, declares war on Russia.

Aug 3—Germany declares war on France.

Aug 4—Russia declares war on Germany. Britain declares war on Germany. Germans enter Belgium to begin fighting.

Aug 6—Austria-Hungary declares war on Russia.

This war set the template for large-scale conflict that continues to this day. Paul and his family—all our families, past and present—continue to be caught up in its dynamics.

Telegraph, telephones, and radio allowed news to travel long distance quickly, ushering in a new era of almost instantaneous decision-making with far-reaching consequences. Ordinary people were turned into breathless and anxious audiences.

With hints of what was to come later in the century, the war was fought first with propaganda campaigns. Germany emphasized nationalism and patriotism, highlighting themes of national unity and defense of the fatherland. They demonized the enemy, especially the British and French, as barbaric and uncivilized. Propaganda often depicted the war as a struggle between the "superior" German culture and the "inferior" cultures of the Allies. This narrative was used to instill a sense of pride and moral righteousness among the German populace.

People of German origin were already at this time a big part of the United States population, and the Kaiser's war had many adherents in the American public, media, and government itself. This caused Congress to elect to stay out of the war through the worst of it, entering only in 1918, four years after it began, but then playing a decisive role in the Allied victory.

Newsreel (1915)

—**British ocean liner Lusitania sunk by German submarine, 1,195 perish.**

–Genocide of estimated 600,000 to 1 million Armenians by Turkish soldiers.

This was a nasty, bloody war on all the fronts.

The industrial revolution accelerated major innovation in military weaponry. When the war began, armies used mounted cavalry brandishing swords on fine horses, until they were replaced by mechanized, armored tanks on treads that tore up the farmlands and forests. The technology of artillery had advanced to allow hurling exploding projectiles hundreds of meters downrange. There was still plenty of glorious hand-to-hand fighting in hand-dug trenches, now supported by the skills of scientists who had harnessed poison gases thrown in cannisters from one enemy army to another. Tens of thousands of innocent young men huddled in trenches for weeks and months at a time, through winter and mud, dying of more conditions than the world had ever experienced before. Or afterwards, life-long "shell shock," the earlier name for post-traumatic stress disorder.

The war at home — Living near the front

Paul was seven years old when those guns of August signaled the onset of war and death. In 1914 he was just beginning school at *Vorschule beim Städtischen Schiller* ("Schiller Municipal Elementary School") and was eleven when the Central powers agreed to cease hostilities, impressionable years for a boy that age. Köln was close to the front during the entire war, so close that in the days just before the Kaiser fled, British forces marched in and occupied Köln.

During the war itself, Paul's father Ernst served as a *Feld Arzt* ("medical field doctor"), shown here in uniform. It's very possible he did this work from his own clinic, and from the Severins Klösterchen Hospital nearby. Perhaps the guns could be heard in the distance, and certainly ambulances were a frequent sight in the city.

Dr. Ernst Mayer as Field Doctor in the Great War

If Paul was like others his age, he followed the action on a map on the wall or kept a scrapbook of news clippings. And he was most likely proud that his papa was a Field Doctor, later decorated for his service to the Kaiser and the fatherland, even while a bloody and catastrophic war raged nearby.

An unusual telling of a young German boy's mind during the Great War comes from Sebastian Haffner in his fascinating book, *Defying Hitler*, written in 1939, an autobiography in which the writer is exactly Paul's age. His chums are all excited about the Great War as it unfolds and collapses, posting large maps for their walls from the day's news showing daily troop movement. But because they never actually saw real action anywhere close to them, they were insulated from the real pain of war, and shocked when it was declared over way before it seemed warranted. Later, with the advent of Nazism, these young men were the most enthusiastic about the glories to come.[2] The question is whether Paul shared any of that excitement.

The Kaiser's Imperial forces, try as they might, were unable to advance further west than they'd achieved in the first months, held back by the Allied forces. And try as they might, the opposing Allied forces were unable to advance further East into Prussia, held back by the Kaiser's Imperial forces. With all this deadly pushing, the front barely moved for most of the war. Stalemate doesn't mean nothing happened, plenty happened. Hundreds of thousands of young men died or were mutilated.

Is it possible this great war was not discussed around Paul's dinner table as a child? Was there no discussion of his father going off to treat the wounded? No discussion of Papa's own encounters with violence? No discussion of his beautiful field uniform? If all this was not discussed, Paul grew up learning not to discuss such things. But surely both he and his family felt something, at some internal gnawing level. The children of horror often grow up in such deafening silence.

Newsreel (1917–1918)

April—First U.S. combat troops arrive in France as US declares war on Germany.

July-Aug—Third Battle of Ypres is fought, and the Second Battle of the Marne.

November—Russian revolutionaries execute the former czar and his family. Russian Civil War between Reds (Bolsheviks) and Whites (anti-Bolsheviks); Reds win in 1920.

---

2   Sebastian Haffner, *Defying Hitler*, written in 1939 but published only in 2000, by Picador Press.

–Worldwide influenza (aka "Spanish flu") pandemic strikes; by 1920, nearly 20 million are dead.

After four years, Germany on its western front was faced with fierce resistance from the British and French Armies, a blockade of supplies to the interior, the entrance of the United States Army, political unrest and starvation at home, an economy in ruins, mutiny in the navy, and mounting defeats on the battlefield. That potent mix spelled defeat.

By November 1918, the military leadership saw that the German Empire was finished, even though-and this proved a point of amazement and disbelief in the ensuing discussions—*even though* the Allies had hardly advanced into German territory. With the prospect of a Socialist revolution growing throughout the homeland, General Paul Von Hindenburg advised Kaiser Wilhelm of the precariousness of his situation and encouraged him to abdicate, which he did on November 9, taking refuge in Holland just over the border.

On November 11, 1918, the day known as "Armistice Day" (changed in the US to Veterans Day by an act of Congress in 1954), German leadership acknowledged military defeat by signing an armistice, a truce signifying the end of armed hostilities, in a railway car at Compiègne northeast of Paris, in a royal forest surrounding the lovely château built by Louis XV and restored by Napoleon for one of his wives.

Under the terms of the Armistice, the German Army was allowed to remain intact and was not forced to admit defeat by surrendering. US General John J. Pershing had misgivings about this, saying it would be better to have the German generals admit defeat so there could be no doubt. The French and British were convinced however that Germany would not be a threat again.

But an armistice is little more than a formalized cease-fire, it doesn't establish a framework for the peace to follow. It took another six months of strenuous and disputed Allied negotiations to produce the all-important Treaty of Versailles, signed eventually on June 28, 1919, in the Palace of Versailles. Debates and disagreements among the victors as to how the vanquished Germans should be treated created a rancorous backdrop that spoiled any chance of a real peace and set the stage for continued discord. The rich Rhineland territories of Alsace and Lorraine were now returned to France, having been taken from her in the Franco-Prussian war concluded fifty years earlier.

From the end of the Great War in 1918 until 1926, the city of Köln was occupied by the British Army of the Rhine under the terms of the Armistice and the subsequent Peace Treaty of Versailles. Young Paul, now an eleven-year-old boy watched the victorious Brits as they rolled into Köln and established an occupation government. He, and Illa too, could have been saddened and they could have been angered, we don't know how they felt or what sort of conversation happened around their breakfast table. Talking about feelings was not a part of the culture of middle-class German families of the time, whether Jewish or Gentile.

Paul comes of age as a stage for the future gets set

Newsreel (1919)

–Versailles Treaty, incorporating Woodrow Wilson's draft Covenant of League of Nations, signed by Allies and Germany. US Senate votes not to join League of Nations.

–Mohandas Gandhi initiates Satyagraha campaigns in India, beginning his nonviolent resistance movement against British rule.

–Race riots erupt in twenty-six U.S. cities during the course of the year, including Washington, DC, Chicago, and Tulsa.

Reviewing the horrors of this war when the damage was fully revealed, the governments left standing felt compelled to push for new rules and arrangements to ensure such an insane outbreak of costly, frenzied war-making would never happen again.

They created the Geneva Conventions to ensure that future wars would be "more humane." They created the International World Court in The Hague to try those charged with war crimes. And they created the League of Nations to be an arbiter of international disputes. Its first substantive task was to register the just concluded Treaty of Versailles. These were enormous and well-intentioned undertakings to support a future of peace. Would they work?

No one wanted to go through such a war again, except for some people who nursed a grudge-quite a few people, actually. Embers from the Great War still smoldered in the rubble and were never extinguished. They continued to smolder, and it wasn't long before they were intentionally fanned, and a small but growing number of people became excited to see their own passion reflected in the growing fire.

It didn't take long, just a few years after going down in defeat, before the labors of Versailles, Geneva, and the Hague were shoved aside and Germanic tribes were at it again: trashing, dehumanizing, imprisoning, bombing, destroying, throwing flame from terrifying machinery, and beating their heroic breasts while marching into foreign capitals as the new supreme power whose bidding shall be done under the banner of skulls and crossbones.

That simple summary of what was on the horizon could be called cartoonish—but not wrong. We know the defeated forces of Germany weren't happy with the Armistice, and with the Treaty of Versailles even less. Many Germans felt sorely aggrieved, even though the terms they were now subjected to in defeat were very similar to what they had imposed on the defeated French following the Franco-Prussian war of 1870, just fifty years earlier.

Beginning almost immediately after the Treaty, people on the political right in Germany and Austria raised their voices in grievance. Resentments and accusations of betrayal began to simmer and roil, with no force adequate to quiet them. Many on the left looked to Russia and its apparently successful Communist Revolution to lead them forward.

***

As for the Mayer family, it survived the war intact and unharmed. Ernst had proudly done his duty to the Fatherland serving as a field doctor, helping to create and lead the new radiology and orthopedic clinic at a Köln hospital, and advancing the state of the clinical art of doctoring the wounded. We can imagine that orthopedic medicine turned out to be a good career choice during a postwar period in which thousands of soldiers had lost their limbs if not their lives.

In 1920, Paul turned thirteen, the age in which boys born into Jewish heritage undertake rigorous preparations for the ritual of *bar mitzvah* (Jewish Babylonian Aramaic for "son of the Commandment") that marks their matriculation to adulthood, when they begin to be held accountable for their own actions. As part of this preparation, Paul was subjected to instruction from Ernst about their lineage, about as close to Talmud Torah education as Paul got.

Ernst and Lisbeth were Liberal Jews, as were their parents and their grandparents. Liberal Judaism ran in the family. Ernst's grandfather, Dr. Rabbi Samuel Mayer introduced many reforms to Jewish observances in the mid-nineteenth century reforms that are foundational to contemporary Reformed Judaism as it's known in the United States. Ernst's father Adolf and his wife Frederiecke (*née* Heidegger) most certainly belonged to a synagogue and attended services along with their three children, at least during high holidays.

Ernst and Lisbeth felt it was important to keep tradition alive and belonged to a synagogue too, though they didn't attend often. And in keeping with the ecumenical tradition of Ernst's ancestors, they also had a *Tannenbaum* ("Christmas tree") that was even lit with real candles.

In any case, while both the Mayer and Teutsch families had many rabbis in their lineage, it seems likely Ernst and Lisbeth moved away from regular weekly rituals as well as celebration of Jewish holidays defined in the calendar. While assimilating to become "German enough," they stayed "Jewish enough" as parents to oversee their son Paul's circumcision, a rite ordained in the Old Testament, symbolizing Jews' compact with God, encourage Paul to undertake the *bar mitzvah* ritual induction into adulthood, and keep to the Prophetic, anti-Zionist line of Liberal Judaism, an attitude passed on to both their children. In any case, it's known that both Ernst and Lisbeth always retained their Jewish identity, in a nominal way at least, until the end.

Evidently Paul felt a duty to his lineage to participate in the ceremony of *bar mitzvah* and become an adult in the Jewish tradition. Paul, of course, had to learn Hebrew, the still-used language of the Jewish service conducted in synagogues throughout the Diaspora when Jews were expelled from Jerusalem in 135 CE and scattered throughout the Roman Empire and across North Africa. He learned enough to recite his assigned reading of the Torah, and years later proudly recalled this accomplishment.

Weimar – Germany comes of age

Germany too was on the threshold of big change. With its Empire collapsed and in ruins, and its military largely decommissioned and dispersed, there were many directions Germany could take. These were all considered loudly in newspapers and cafes throughout the country, with attitudes ranging from despair to optimism and back again.

This was the time, finally, for Germany to try its hand at democracy. Virtually all the powers and former powers of Europe had undertaken some form of it, and conditions seemed right.

In 1918 the powers that be created a republic of former states that had kept their identities intact, joined them together, and put their trust in the people, who at the time were pretty miserable. "Germany" became the Weimar Republic, with the rules for governance written into a newly agreed Weimar Constitution. When the famous "Third Reich," the one that was to last a thousand years, was announced just a few years later, the Weimar Republic became counted as the Second Reich, and Imperial Germany (1871–1918) as the First.

Although late to the party of democratic government, it was eagerly awaited by many as exactly the kind of thing that idealists, intellectuals, and revolutionaries had been demanding for decades, ever since Napoleon had planted the seeds of an enlightened governance.

Unfortunately, it was created against a backdrop of economic hardship affecting many dispirited and defeated people. Factions with very different ideas jockeyed for influence. There were semi-organized groups of veterans of the defeated but once proud military, no longer with a mission, but still identifying with it. Politically, a full range of parties flourished—communists, socialists, democrats, nationalists, capitalists—each with its own factions straining for dominance. Among the parties were the "social democrats," idealists following the innovations in participatory government begun a few decades earlier in the United States and in other western European nations.

Weimar culture—"Weimar" was a culture before it was a government[3]—began before the Great War and captured the high ideals promoted by fans of the American and French revolutions who also proclaimed Germany as the height of civilization. Proponents of the Republic were essentially upbeat, carrying on an intellectual and cultural tradition begun a few decades earlier. Their cultural hero was Johann Wolfgang von Goethe (born 1749 in Frankfurt am Main,

---

3   Walter Laqueur, *Weimar: A Cultural History 1918-1933*, NY: G.P. Putnam's Sons, 1974.

died 1832 in the small town of Weimar), a poet, playwright, novelist, scientist, statesman, theatre director, and critic.

In the 1920s, "the Weimar Republic was a breathless era of cultural flowering that drew the world's attention to German dance, German architecture, German filmmaking, German fiction, German theater, German art and music... The Weimar Republic provided clusters of excitement, akin to Paris around the turn of the century, way out of proportion to the mere fourteen years of its life.[4]"

Paul grew up in this culture, and there's no doubt Paul's public school education at his Gymnasium in Köln reflected the classical values of the early Weimar age. During his eight years at the Schiller Gymnasium (1917-24), he took twenty-four trimesters of Latin, eighteen trimesters of French, fifteen of Greek, six of English, and two of Spanish, as well as German, Religion, Nature studies, Writing, and Math in every term. We have his report cards!

Economic collapse, and Revolution!

The possibilities offered to Paul as he came of age in this new Weimar period were expansive. The world was his oyster. Germany had a new modern government that had possibilities.

Having set sail, the new Weimar Republic quickly found the sea onto which it was launched anything but smooth. The economy of the time went from bad to worse. Its condition was roughly the same as before the war, but with increased poverty and rampant inflation. The rich got richer and the poor got poorer. Refugees suffering from even worse conditions in lands to the east arrived in great numbers, and the cities and entire countryside became increasingly crowded and stressful. Hunger erupted from devastated farm-to-table distribution lines. The times were dire for many.

Germany was not alone in experiencing major collapses in the

---

4 Peter Gay, *Weimar Culture: Outsider as Insider,* Norton, 1968 and 2001.

way things were before the Great War. Even the victorious countries of Europe were stressed. Britain, which lost hundreds of thousands of its "finest generation" in the war, saw the collapse of its culture of aristocracy and the economic infrastructure that supported it (see *Downton Abbey*). France, while delighting in its re-acquisition of Lorraine and Alsace through its victory, also lost hundreds of thousands of its population in the war and saw the collapse of its third republic in less than one hundred years.

***

In April of 1921, the victorious European Allies, notably France and England, presented a bill to Germany demanding payment for damages caused in the Great War, a war which they said Germany had started. This bill for war reparations, amounting to the equivalent of thirty-three billion US dollars even then, had the immediate effect of causing ruinous inflation in Germany. Just how odious were the term of the Treaty has been an ongoing subject of fierce debate, but none of that mattered to those nursing a grievance and a grudge. "Why should we bear all the costs? You can't honestly say we started this war by ourselves, so what about the other losing nations?"

The German currency, the Deutschmark, slipped drastically in value. It had been four marks to the US dollar until the bill for war reparations was announced. Then it became seventy-five to the dollar and in 1922 sank to 400 to the dollar. The German government asked for a postponement of payments. The French refused. The Germans defied them by defaulting on their payments. In response to this, in January of 1923, the French Army occupied the Ruhr Valley, the industrial heart of Germany.

Hyper-inflation of the Deutschmark ran through Germany like a highly contagious virus. The German mark fell to 18,000 to the dollar. By July 1923, it sank to 160,000. By August, 1,000,000, and by November 1923 it took 4,000,000,000 marks to buy a dollar.

Germans lost their life savings. Salaries were paid in worthless money. Groceries cost billions. Hunger riots broke out.

This stressed everyone, which of course included the patients seen by Dr. Mayer. Some were still able to pay in currency, but the value of their Deutschmarks decreased by the minute. Some could pay their bill from their garden in the country, with butter, eggs, or sausage. But the legal currency was in freefall. After receiving payment for an office visit, Ernst would immediately hand the money to the housekeeper and direct her to run to the market before the Deutschmark dropped any further. This was still a few years before the US, still experiencing the glories of the Roaring '20s, suffered its disastrous 1929 collapse of its stock market and the ensuing Depression felt around the world.

Paul watched all this with a growing interest in economics and political science. Years later, he told us that an idea took shape around the family table, an idea based on his grandfather Adolf's life. While himself quite young, Adolf Mayer, encouraged by his father Rabbi Samuel Mayer, emigrated to the United States where economic prospects were likely better than those of rural Baden-Württemberg of the 1850s. He went to Toledo, Ohio in 1854 where he had distant relatives on his mother's side. When the US Civil War broke out Adolf enlisted in the US Army with the 27th Ohio Volunteers, Company B. This unit saw considerable action, marching and fighting up and down the Mississippi River valley. At some point he was wounded in action and transferred to a position as an Army paymaster in St. Louis and also became a US citizen while his unit traveled further south and eventually east to Savannah following the Union's march to the sea. While in St. Louis, he was invited and encouraged to return home to Germany where he could join family recently settled in Trier.

Paul suggested that because Adolf had been a US citizen and Army veteran he was probably entitled to a pension. A pension from the US government could mean a great deal if its benefits could now go to Adolf's descendants. Although Adolf had died in 1907, his widow, Frederiecke, was still alive in 1923, and Ernst encouraged her to write a letter to the US State Department, and to send all the supporting paperwork she had at her disposal. And miracle of miracles, a pension was granted, and even better, it was paid out with US dollars, a much more secure currency at the time than the Deutschmark. The princely sum of thirty dollars was distributed monthly to Ernst's account (and presumably to the accounts of his mother and sisters Lottie and Thea as well). This was a substantial sum that greatly helped his family's survival during this period, Paul later said.

Newsreel (1922-1924)

—Mussolini marches on Rome, forms Fascist government.

—Lincoln Memorial is dedicated in Washington, D.C.

—Adolf Hitler's "Beer Hall Putsch" in Munich fails; in 1924 he is sentenced to five years in prison where he writes Mein Kampf. He is released after eight months.

—The second Ku Klux Klan movement in U.S. history grows, stirring widespread controversy and violence.

For the moment, the German people stood by their government, admiring its defiance of the French. But in September of 1923, the Weimar Republic made a fateful decision to resume making payments on their bill of reparations for its role in destroying much of Europe. Bitter resentment and unrest swelled among the people, inciting extremist political groups to action and quickly bringing Germany to the brink of chaos.

Enter the still-small right-wing National Socialist German Workers' Party (abbreviated as "Nazi"), led by thirty-four-year-old Adolf Hitler since 1921. Despite having the term Socialist in its name, the National Socialist German Workers' Party was a right-wing party. In a stroke of brilliant marketing, Hitler had made these words mean what he wanted them to mean, and he meant pro-nationalist, anti-capitalist, anti-communist, anti-bourgeois. He could sell it with changing nuance over time.

Hitler had served in the Army of the German Empire (not the Austro-Hungarian Empire of his homeland) as a messenger on the Western front. He had seen its horrors, but instead of resolving "never again," resolved instead to nurse and activate the sense of shame and bitterness he experienced with the defeat of his adopted country. Even by this point in his life, he embraced three principles essential to his own party and politics: organizing, propaganda, and terror.[5]

The National Socialist party, along with other similar groups on the political right now felt the time was right to strike against its still-new national government-to topple it in a *putsch* ("*coup d'état*" in French). The German state of Bavaria where the Nazis were based was a hotbed of groups opposed to the democratic government in Berlin. By November 1923, the Nazis, with 55,000 followers, were the biggest and best organized of right-wing parties. With Nazi members demanding action, Hitler knew he must act or risk losing the Party's leadership.

Hitler and the Nazis hatched a plot in which they would kidnap the leaders of the Bavarian government and force them at gunpoint to accept Hitler as their leader. Then, according to their plan, with the aid of the Prussian war leader General Erich Ludendorff, they would win over the German army, proclaim a nationwide revolt and bring down the German democratic government in Berlin.

They put this plan into action when they learned there was to be a large gathering of businessmen in a Munich beer hall and the guests of honor were to be the Bavarian leaders they wanted to kidnap.

---

5   The history of Hitler, the Nazis, and Nazi Germany is thoroughly told by William Shirer in *The Rise and Fall of the Third Reich: A History of Nazi Germany*, 1960, Simon and Schuster.

On November 8, 1923, Nazi *Sturmabteilung* (abbreviated SA., commonly translated as "Storm Troopers), the paramilitary wing of the Party under the direction of Hermann Göring surrounded the beer hall. At 8:30 pm. Hitler and his storm troopers burst into the beer hall causing instant panic. Hitler fired a pistol shot into the ceiling. "Silence!" he yelled at the stunned crowd. Hitler and Göring forced their way to the podium as armed SA men continued to file into the hall. State Commissioner Gustav von Kahr, whose speech had been interrupted by all this, yielded the podium to Hitler.

"The National Revolution has begun!" Hitler shouted, in what became known as the Beer-Hall Putsch.

As soon as Hitler shouted this, he heard "You're under arrest!" He was then charged with seditious treason, tried, convicted, and sentenced to five years of solitary confinement in Spandau Prison in west Berlin. Thanks to a lenient system, he served only a few months.

While these events were national news, the Nazi party was still only a minor party. More importantly, Germany continued to operate under the provisions of the Weimar Constitution, which permitted multiple parties and was working well enough. The threat (or promise) posed by Hitler's proclamation of a national revolution seemed contained. He was in jail, after all, on the serious charge of seditious treason.

Hitler in prison: *"Mein Kampf"*

While in jail, Hitler wrote a book that shaped his public rhetoric in the years to come. He himself didn't write it, of course, he dictated it to Rudolf Hess, also imprisoned for his part in the Putsch and a life-long deputy of Hitler. They both relished their roles. Hitler titled it, *Mein Kampf* ("My Struggle"), and had it published in July 1925.

In it, Hitler described the struggle for world domination, a subject evidently important to him, as an ongoing racial, cultural, and political battle between Aryans—his name for the "Master Race"—

and Jews (informally known amongst themselves as "the chosen people," but never as a political platform, and kicked around for centuries).

To explain the collapse of the glorious German Empire and its glorious military, Hitler put forward the thesis it was caused by a stab in the back by "the Jews." I say "the Jews" because in the rhetoric of the day Jews are grouped as a group, so all Jews were guilty by association. He accused "the Jews" of conducting an international conspiracy to control world finances, inventing Marxism in addition to liberal democracy, controlling the press, and also promoting prostitution and vice. Promoting capitalism and communism at the same time were not seen by Hitler or his base as a contradiction, because "the Jews," he said, are a single entity that "uses culture to spread disharmony."

Blaming the Jews for social ills wasn't new. It went back to the earliest days of German Christianity. But as Germany became increasingly Nazified, the notion of a conspiracy of Jews bent on destroying the German Empire was incorporated into the state's official beliefs. From there it was a short jump to the requirement that it be taught in the schools, ignoring the many other explanations for German defeat.

Hitler's attitude toward "the Jews" would become shared to varying degrees by millions of Germans, which to be consistent should be more directly called "the Christians." Those reluctant to embrace the emerging Nazi ideology of violent antisemitism either remained silent or felt little choice but to participate actively in the Nazi's mission, not fully expressed yet, to rid Europe of Jews from one end to the other. "Getting rid of the Jews" had not yet been publicly translated as "exterminating the Jews," but it soon would be.

Mein Kampf also provided a narrative to support the military conquests Hitler later embraced once he had himself installed as dictator of Germany, an aspiration he always had, says Shirer. Hitler stated that since the Aryans are the master race, they were entitled simply by that fact to acquire more land for themselves. This "living space" (*Lebensraum*) included the lands populated by Slavic people, the lands just east and south of Germany (Poland, the Balkans, Ukraine, Russia, etc.), was to be acquired by force, Hitler said. That land would be used to cultivate food and provide land and recreation opportunities for the expanding Aryan population—at the expense of the Slavic peoples, who were also considered in the Nazi ideology to be inferior and were to be enslaved or removed.

When *Mein Kampf* was first released in 1925 it was not an immediate hit, and in fact it sold poorly even among his comrades from the days of the attempted coup. Hitler's still-small base of supporters had been hoping for a juicy autobiography or a behind-the-scenes story of the Beer Hall Putsch. What they got were hundreds of pages of long, hard-to-follow sentences and wandering paragraphs composed by an ill-behaved man on a rant.

The book itself languished until after Hitler became Chancellor of Germany eight years later in 1933. It would then become *de rigeur* to present a copy as a gift to newlyweds or school graduates, or to celebrate any similar occasion.

While Hitler couldn't write well, he sure could speak, and he began to attract big crowds through his forceful oratory. Shivers still run down the spines of those who witnessed the sound, even on the radio. It was personal, vengeful, and delivered to the gut.

***

In the years following the Great War, Paul lived with his parents and sister Illa in a handsome home that also contained Ernst's medical practice, which was doing quite well. The building, at Friesenplatz 12, was in a lively residential neighborhood. It wasn't in the physical remnants of Jewish Köln because Ernst's family evidently didn't feel connected enough to the Jewish community to live there.

Paul might have been paying attention to current affairs, as it's very likely his father read the daily paper, and probably in front of the children. In any case, the Newsreels I've provided as well as my "introduction to the social and political history of the German-speaking world" is meant to provide the reader with enough, perhaps more than enough, context to appreciate Paul's world.

Friesenplatz 12, Köln, home and office of Dr. Ernst Mayer and family

Paul finished his studies at the *Vorschule beim Städtischen Schiller Gymnasium* in 1926, which he'd entered in 1917. A German "gymnasium" has no relation to an American gymnasium, but is the rough equivalent of American high school but with higher academic standards akin to those for the "college bound" in the US. He did well enough to recognize that his future probably involved more schooling, but he was in no hurry to make the leap.

Paul was living a comfortable, privileged life with a bright though unplanned future. He grew up expecting others to do things for him, at least in affairs of his own maintenance. It was said that his mother buttered his morning bread, and his father bought him his first car. He had school chums. The Mayers always had a dog or two, always dachshunds. He and Illa were close, and both really loved the "*Dackel.*"

Ernst and Lisbeth and their two children enjoyed occasional weekends and perhaps longer at a modest hunting cabin in the Eifel Mountains southeast of Köln on a piece of land on the Kall River known as "*Zweifallshammer.*" It's possible they owned it, perhaps part of the legacy of Ernst's mother Frederiecke who came from nearby, or perhaps it was made available to him through his affiliation with the Severins Klösterchen Hospital in Köln. I suggest this because also on this property were two substantial two-story half-timbered buildings from the turn of the century that had been used as a medical facility during the Great War.

Both Paul and Illa described pleasant and exciting weekends there with their parents. Ernst loved tramping around the river bottoms, Paul learned to hunt and shoot game birds, and Illa developed a love for the wild animals there.

"Zweifallshammer," hunting cabin of Dr. Ernst Mayer family in Eifel Mountains, early 1930s

Paul loved telling the story of how one day Illa, then eleven, went missing from the lodge's grounds, and a small posse was assembled to search the surrounding dense forest. After several hours they returned empty-handed and apprehensive, only to find Illa standing inside the fencing of the cabin's corral alongside a ferocious-looking wild boar that had been captured the day before. Illa was gently stroking its snout, and the boar seemed quite content.

It would have helped this story, and my understanding of Paul in his early years, if he'd ever spoken of his adventures, anxieties, and trials as a youngster and adolescent. We know he played lots of tennis. He was good, too, winning a city-wide tournament in his age group, and developing his competitive nature. He also got his driver's license, and there was talk of a girlfriend.

We're left with the understanding of him as privileged, bright, athletic, competitive, engaging, and socially fit young man of the times.

Paul stakes a path

Not long after graduation, Paul decided to become a lawyer. How he came to this decision isn't clear, but he was probably working up to it. The pressure to do something with his life was presumably on. He knew he couldn't just play tennis and enjoy the annual Karnival. His mother thought his girlfriend "unsuitable." He still lived at home with his parents and Illa and spent time with friends from school or the neighborhood.

Even though his father's medical practice was secure and his reputation was significant, Paul didn't want to follow in his footsteps. A career in Law, however, had possibilities. It would provide respectability, income sufficient to support a family in comfort, travel in interesting circles, and access to a number of productive vocational callings.

Plus, there were exemplary precedents in both his father's and mother's family line. Paul's maternal grandfather Julius Teutsch had been a prominent attorney in Metz, Lorraine until it fell into French hands in the Great War, driving him back to Köln, safely within Germany. As a young man Paul knew his Opa Julius well, and they liked each other. Opa Julius encouraged Paul to consider taking up Law.

And there was the well-known precedence in the Mayer line. Paul's paternal great-grandfather Samuel was not only a rabbi but also a lawyer, the first rabbi in Germany ever to hold both credentials, in 1849. In his studies and later writing he was what's now called a social justice or human rights lawyer and contributed mightily to the development of that field's principles. He became famous for creating a stupendous three-volume work called, in English, *The rights of the Israelites, Athenians and Romans, with regard to the new legislation, for jurists, statesmen, theologians, philologists, philosophers and historians presented in parallel.* "A contribution," Rabbi Mayer called it, "to a system and to a history of universal law— which was highly influential in its day."

We can imagine Paul taking note of this family and social history and becoming seriously convinced by the possibilities of a career in law. In any case, his choice of a career in law was a good one. It certainly marked his life, his career, and the occupations afforded him from then on. If he'd chosen medicine, or tennis, his entire future would have been different. He made his move.

He began his law studies at the University of Köln in 1926. He then took and passed state exams in commercial and labor law, securities law, taxation, and national economics. He also studied in Berlin, Geneva, and Paris in the period 1927 and 1928. In 1929, he became *Referendar* (like a legal intern, a necessity in the training of German lawyers), in the firm of Lissauer & Co., a large minerals and manufacturing company in Köln. In November 1931 he received a doctorate in law and economics from the Law Faculty of University of Köln.

***

Newsreel (1929)

First large-scale Jewish-Arab violence caused by a clash at the Wailing Wall in Jerusalem.

Stock market prices plummet (Nov.-Dec.). U.S. securities lose twenty-six billion dollars, marking the first financial disaster of the Great Depression

Newsreel (1930)

September 14—Germans elect Nazis in sufficient number to make them the second-largest political party in Germany.

Raus, Juden! Raus mit ihnen! ("Get out, Jews! Out with you!")

Paul began to hear this on the street. *Raus, Juden!* ("Get out, Jews!"). They weren't yelling at him, he thought, they were yelling at those Eastern Jews who'd recently arrived impoverished and didn't speak German, didn't have soft-boiled eggs for breakfast with his toast buttered, and hadn't lived in Germany for countless generations contributing to the Fatherland. He was convinced of that. And throughout his time studying law, Paul was steadfast in that pursuit.

There are only a few stories of him being distracted. In one, he lost his tuition money in a poker game just before the semester began. He apparently wasn't shy about wiring home for more, and it came.

With a bit of envy, he told of attending fraternity parties of the very non-Jewish kind, with saber duels and slashed cheeks. These were popular with the sons of the former nobility and officer corps that made up postwar fraternities. Also, among his possessions that I inherited was a bound book of German drinking songs, the binding stuck with substantial brass studs so it could sit high and dry above the beer sloshing on the table itself. He wished, it seems in later reporting, that he could belong.

Berlin at the time was a hotbed of *avant garde* cultural activity, offering plenty of ways to be distracted from study. Theater, cabaret, art, music, literature, poetry—all were undergoing exciting development and change, rivalling and even exceeding the glory days of Paris thirty years earlier, where *"avant garde"* was invented. Exciting as it may have been, Paul seems to have passed it by. I never knew him to be particularly interested in the hip cultural scene, except Simon and Garfunkel, he liked them. He also said once that he liked the swing jazz of the '30s, but I never noticed him listen to it.

Berlin was also a hotbed of politics—extreme left, center left, center, center right, and extreme right, with shades in-between. Paul could, as large numbers of students have always done, pick up the cause of left-wing politics, but he did not. He seemed determined not to be politicized.

In 1930, Paul wrote a doctoral dissertation on the Prussian penal system, *The prison system in stages. According to the Prussian state's 'Regulation of the penal system in stages, from 7 June 1929.'* One can't help but note just from the title its similarity to his great-grandfather's three-volume book. But why he chose to write about the penal system isn't clear. Criminal law was never a real interest before or after this time, but a comparative analysis like this does mirror his great-grandfather's approach.

In 1931, Paul published his seventy-nine page doctoral dissertation in Köln in support of his degree of Doctor of Laws. He specialized, he noted years later, in "commercial and international law." And in November, he was granted Doctor of Law from the Law Faculty of University of Köln.

He still kept his nose to the grindstone and undertook more studies to become an *Assessor.* This is a title held by graduates of law who have passed both the first and the second of the two state exams (finishing law school and a two-year legal clerkship) qualifying for a career in a legal profession such as judge or prosecutor, attorney at law or civil-law notary.

Newsreel (1932)

July–The Nazis win 230 governmental seats. Together with the Communists, the next largest party, they make up over half of the Reichstag.

November–Franklin Roosevelt elected President of the United States for first time.

From Nazi ascendance to dictatorial control

The year 1932 saw Hitler's meteoric rise to prominence in Germany. It was spurred largely by the German people's frustration with dismal economic conditions caused in part by the now global Depression, the still-festering emotional wounds inflicted by defeat of the invincible German nation in the Great War, and the harsh peace terms of the Versailles treaty. A charismatic speaker, Hitler channeled popular discontent with the post-war Weimar government into support for his growing Nazi party.

The economy was still weak, and the Weimar government too weak to manage it. Volatility in the markets was fearsome, as were the opinions on what to do about it. Political parties on the right saw the risk of communism or socialism rising bigger than ever in the East, threatening to wash over them in the West. The euphoria of "national unity" that prevailed in 1914 just before the Great War still coursed through the veins of German nationalists.[6]

---

6   See Peter Fritzsche, *Germans Into Nazis*, 1998, Harvard University Press.

Many historians now see the faulty military and diplomatic ending to the Great War, as well as the unstable ground under the Weimar Republic, as the inevitable beginning of the next disaster-a steady progression from "World War I" to "World War II."

This rising revolutionary tide from the left was coming primarily from Russia, where the struggle for a communist/socialist/Marxist social-economic system was the most advanced. But it was rising in almost every other country whose prosperity as well as its poverty was rooted in the economic disparities created by rising industrialization.

**

Everything changed in 1933. In January, Hitler took full control of all government. In March, he was given dictatorial power. And then-just look at this newsreel. What leaps out? Everything!

Newsreel (1933)

January 30–Adolf Hitler becomes Chancellor of Germany, leader of not just his party but the entire nation.

February 27–The German Reichstag burns, emboldening the new Nazi administration to respond with violence.

March 23–The Enabling Act gives Hitler dictatorial power, allowing him to put the courts and the military under him, not alongside him.

April 1–Hitler orders a boycott of Jewish owned shops.

May 10–Hitler authorizes book burning throughout Germany.

June–Germany opens Dachau concentration camp near Munich. It's presented as a deterrent for political dissidents and becomes a training ground for SS guards who were later deployed to later extermination camps. It was not an extermination camp as such. It specialized in political prisoners, and more of these were murdered in Dachau than in any other camp.

Hitler's National Socialist party didn't win the July 1932 election with a decisive majority, and in November the Nazis even lost thirty-five seats. But the powers that be feared Communism even more than the Nazis, so on January 30, President Paul von Hindenburg named Adolf Hitler, leader (*"führer"*) of the National Socialist Party, to be Chancellor of Germany, the top executive position.

The year 1933 was a happy one for everyone officially deemed German patriots who saw themselves favored by the Nazi agenda. For those not included and explicitly excluded from Nazi favor, there was government-sponsored harassment, with increasing menace over time.

"Increasing menace over time" is a key phrase in that last sentence. Nothing happened overnight but in a steady progression of menace ratcheting ever tighter and closer, lasting six full years before Hitler led Germany into war with the world, eight full years before full-scale implementation of the "final solution," and twelve full years before his vision and he himself were fully crushed. All this ratcheting happened in full sight, not just in Germany but throughout the world—but the menace was too often ignored.

On the list of those excluded from the beneficence of the Nazi program: anyone belonging to political parties to the left of the Nazis, and since the National Socialist party was on the far right, this was a large number. And most famously, "the Jews." This meant *all* Jews, not just communist Jews, not just capitalist Jews, not just patriotic Jews, and certainly not just Jews recently immigrating from the East, but *all* Jews, even those whose roots in Germany went back centuries, even those who had served the fatherland as recently as the last war.

There was a "Jewish problem," the Nazis said, "and we must be rid of the Jews." If Jews were such a problem in Germany, one might wonder just how big a portion of the population they were. From the sound of the mobs and the Nazi party, one might think Jews were at least twenty percent of the population. Not even close.

Fifteen percent? Ten? Actually, in January 1933 there were some 523,000 Jews in Germany, representing *less than one percent* of the country's total population. About one-third of German Jews lived in Berlin, constituting less than two and a half percent of the that city's population. By comparison: Poland then had a population of 3,325,000 (10.3 percent Jewish), and Soviet Union 3,020,000 (1.8 percent Jewish). [7]

Hollywood has led us to believe it was only the Jews that the Nazis hated. Not so. Beginning with Hitler's installation in 1933 as Chancellor with no Constitution other than his own, his Party (i.e., his Government) proclaimed one policy after another against various groups deemed "enemies of the state." This included lefties of all stripes: Gypsies, homosexuals, people with disabilities—all rounded up, concentrated in newly opened camps like Dachau outside Munich or other facilities—sometimes released, sometimes castrated, sometimes sterilized, sometimes experimented upon, sometimes worse.

But also included among the excluded, for whom no living space was to be planned in the grand project of National Socialism, were homeless people, single mothers, large poor families, the long-term unemployed, and sex workers.[8]

***

In the midst of this progression—who can know how far this or any progression goes while it's still in progress?—good things can and do happen.

We can imagine this celebratory scene in Ernst's home, set on March 23, on the occasion of Paul's admission to the bar of the High Court of Köln.

---

7   The lion's share of the six million Jews exterminated in the ensuing war were not from Germany but from surrounding countries, especially those further east and southeast.

8   From the brochure of the exhibition, *De Zwarte Driehoek (The Black Triangle) The history of those persecuted as anti-social, 1933-1945*, Vrijheidsmuseum, Netherlands

Ernst hands Paul a glass of champagne with the family gathered around—Lisbeth, Illa, Paul's grandfather Julius Teutsch, the one who promoted to Paul the idea of a career in Law—and possibly one or two of the Teutsch cousins in Köln.

"*Paulchen*, if I may still call you *Paulchen*, you are to be congratulated for this significant accomplishment! You began your law studies just four years ago, passed all your exams, didn't lose too much at poker, and stayed clear of major distractions. Just look at this beautiful diploma, signed by the Faculty of Law, University of Köln, Granted 6 November 1931. And now you've been admitted to the bar of the High Court in Köln, the highest level of legitimacy conferred in the legal profession. From here you can contribute to life as a true patriotic German! You have my most sincere and heartfelt congratulations!"

Everyone applauds.

"Not so fast, Jew."

On the very same day as this well-deserved celebration, news of the most dismaying kind arrived from Berlin. The newly elected members of the German Parliament (the *Reichstag*) met to consider passing Hitler's all-important "Enabling Act." Becoming Chancellor of Germany with the *Reischstag* in support was not enough for Herr Hitler, as it didn't give him full control of everything, and *Reischstag* deliberations can take time. If the Enabling Act passed, it would literally end the experiment with democracy in Germany, end the Constitution of the Weimar Republic, end the Republic itself, establish the legal dictatorship of Adolf Hitler, and begin the countdown for the Thousand Year Third Reich.

Just before the vote, Hitler made a speech to the Reichstag in which he pledged to use restraint. He also promised an end to unemployment and pledged to promote peace with France, Great Britain and the Soviet Union. But to do all this, Hitler said, he first needed the Enabling Act.

A vote was taken: 444 in favor, and 94 against, and 109 "absent." Most of those "absent" had been arrested or were in hiding.

"On this day, March 23, 1933, the Enabling Act establishes the power of the Nazi-led government to pass law by decree, bypassing the approval of parliament. This law hereby nullifies the Weimar Constitution. From this day of the Enabling Act forward, the popularly elected *Reichstag* will become, in effect, just a sounding board, a cheering section for *der Führer*. The democratic ideals of the Weimar Republic are hereby officially squashed." The Supreme Court did not object.

The Nazis achieved what Hitler had wanted for years, to tear down the German Democratic Republic. While he was not elected by the people of Germany to this, it can also be said he used the tools of democracy to destroy democracy and implement autocracy. He was not directly elected to this position of Dictator, or even Chancellor. He did this legally through a vote of the Reichstag but not through a vote of the people. This enabled the complete takeover of Germany by the National Socialists and its leader, Adolf Hitler.

This was the moment of the official collapse of constitutional government in Germany, and the official installation of dictatorial authority.

Paul, having himself just arrived at the doorway to his intended future, was stopped in his tracks.

***

To demonstrate the values of the new government and to recognize the power of the written word and the ideas behind them, books written by people the dictatorship didn't like were publicly burned, even those popular with a wide German readership. On April 8, the Office on Press and Propaganda of the German Student Union proclaimed a nationwide "Action against the Un-German Spirit," to climax in a nationwide burning of books by Jewish or democratic authors. On May 10, the German nation gathered around nighttime campfires in their communities to witness this literary and spirited "cleansing by fire."

Next, "Your citizenship is in jeopardy," read the coming edicts. In the first months after Hitler got sole control of the government, the Weimar laws governing citizenship were dramatically altered. Jews were increasingly excluded from the rights of citizenship, beginning with the Citizenship and Denaturalization Law passed in July 1933. The law allowed the government to take away the citizenship of those who were deemed "undesirable," applying to anyone given citizenship by the Weimar government. Those who saw the results of this law first, in 1933, were the 150,000 Eastern Jews in Germany.

"Raus! You're done here, Jew!"

Then in April, the Law for the Restoration of the Professional Civil Service, or "Civil Service Law," as it was more commonly known when passed, declared this:

"With this law we declare the Nazi-led government can legally remove undesirables (defined as non-Aryans, among others) from the civil service profession, including doctors, teachers and lawyers.

"With this law, Jews are no longer allowed to practice medicine within the extensive government-supported health systems, or law within the government's civil service or judicial systems. Also, all non-Aryans are to retire from the legal profession and civil service.

This law directly affected both Ernst and Paul. It affected Paul immediately, but Ernst and other honored veterans of the Great War were given exemptions, at least for a while.

In June, Paul's admission to the bar at the High Court in Köln was canceled by decree of the Ministry of Justice, "because he was not of Aryan descent." He returned his judicial robes in their original wrapping, unused.

Just like that, by dictatorial powers, Paul's years of study, his success with exams, his published dissertation, and all his legal standing before the bar were nullified. *Raus!* "From now on, you Jews are no longer allowed to practice law in our courtrooms anymore. Why? Because you're Jewish." Paul's great grandfather Samuel turned over in his grave. Almost one hundred years of equality of citizenship erased.

Paul's father was similarly abused, which was perhaps even worse because his entire lifetime of accomplishment and contribution to Germany was erased through the new laws of the Nazis, including his most treasured accomplishments.

Not just his years of service during the Great War serving the Kaiser. This was bigger—his work to create the Radiology Department of the Severins Klösterchen Hospital more than twenty-five years earlier, at the very beginning of this new medical science. In his honor, the hospital had commissioned a life-sized portrait of Ernst and presented it to him at the twenty fifth anniversary of this department, which hung in a prominent place at this hospital.

But the new laws directed the Severins Klösterchen Hospital to remove his portrait. No more legitimizing the contributions of a Jew, they said. Ernst had no choice but to carry this portrait home with him. Both he and the portrait were banned.

"I had not seen my father as deeply moved," Paul recounted to an old friend years later, "as when he came home from the hospital in 1933 with a life size portrait of him that was just removed from the hospital's portrait gallery, as he himself was, a portrait that had been made of Ernst and presented to him in a jubilee ceremony in honor of twenty-five years of service."

Perhaps worse, Paul even witnessed this humiliation of his father. Such sights are difficult to unsee. It is remarkable that he shared this memory with his oldest friend. Neither Ernst nor Paul were men who expressed emotion, not even with each other, even when these anti-Jewish directives stripped both of them of their livelihoods and subjected them to constant public humiliation and harassment in the

Germany they both loved.

Paul apparently didn't see this coming, or didn't believe it could come to his own doorstep. This may be the hardest thing to understand from the vantage point of years later, though it's clear with hindsight. Perhaps his own sense of disbelief clouded his view of the future. Paul had thought, deep in his heart, that the Nazi policy of anti-Semitism was simply not directed at him, a German who was Jewish, but a German nevertheless. It was meant for non-German Jews, those poor newcomers flooding across the eastern border, the ones that apparently fed the Nazi stereotype of what Jews are like. The Jews Paul knew had lived in Germany for generations, were educated and successful as they assimilated into the liberal national context that had been emerging for several generations. Clearly this no longer mattered in the eyes of the new law or the new government. They were Jews.

What to do?

So, big question: Now that the dictatorial Nazi regime had stripped both Paul and his father of their certifications to serve the State in their professional capacities, depriving them of their usual means to support their families, what can they each do?

Paul began to consider options.

Could he align with the Nazi power? Certainly not. As a Jew he would not legally have been permitted. Stories abound of Jews trying to "pass" as non-Jews, often not even knowing they are legally and officially Jewish, and meeting a terrible fate.

Could he fight the power? Not legally, not since democracy was toppled. It would have to be through violence, which is hard to imagine, given the government's momentum and its armed force. Private ownership of firearms *by anyone* had been severely restricted even in the Weimar years, and in 1933 the police were given broad powers to inspect homes.

Could he leave? Yes, but where could he go? At this point he had options: Great Britain, the United States, Palestine, parts of

Asia, Antarctica perhaps. While these were permitted options, they each seemed too remote, and none of those really called to him. And he was a German who loved his country, dammit! Turns out he wasn't German enough.

Paul was encouraged by his maternal grandfather, Julius Teutsch, his "Opa," to seek opportunity to practice law outside Germany. Paul first considered England, though it would mean beginning law studies anew, as the English system is quite different. France offered greater possibilities, where the Napoleonic system of law is similar to that practiced in Germany.

Paul felt tossed in the wind, a whole new unconsidered world that he didn't really want to consider. Just four years earlier, in the face of limitless opportunity, he had set out to make himself a lawyer and establish himself as his own man with prospects. But as quickly as he finally grasped the gold ring, it was snatched away. "Not so fast, Jew." And now his world of opportunity was not limitless in the slightest, but quite limited. What could happen next? Nothing that he could imagine.

This was all in the first year of the dictatorship. Sympathizers as well as opponents far and wide marveled at what this new government could do.

Paul gets lucky

In June 1933, Paul decided to visit Paris to see what he could see. The young man with a shiny new diploma in hand must have felt somewhat hopeful. He hoped to draw on his Opa's French connections from his earlier days in Metz, but Opa too was disenfranchised by the Nazi decrees. At least being in Paris gave Paul a sense of safe distance from Nazi Germany. There was a solid border between those two countries, and he could always go home for a visit.

He rented an apartment in the heart of the Latin Quarter. His French skills were reasonably good, and he began to learn his way around. It was Spring, it was Paris, and everyone knows of the potency of that mix.

Soon after Paul's arrival in Paris in June 1933, new restrictions on German Jews traveling outside the country were announced from the government in Berlin. Feeling a bit unsettled, Paul sought advice on what these new rules might mean to him, and went to *l'Agence pour les Droits de l'Hommes* ("Agency for Human Rights.")

A beautiful young woman entered just ahead of Paul. Paul instinctively got in line right behind her, and was able to overhear bits of the conversation she had with the clerk. Obviously shaken by what the clerk told her, she began to leave. Apparently forgetting why he himself had come, Paul thoughtfully approached her. He touched her sleeve and said, "I don't think your situation is as dire as *monsieur* suggests. I'm here for the same reason as you are, but I'm a lawyer with some knowledge of these issues. How about you and I get out of this place and go have a drink somewhere and discuss the possibilities. How about that cafe just over there?"

"Paul gave me his card," recounted the lovely Margarete ("Margo") Koch years later. "It said, 'Dr. Paul Mayer, Attorney at the Supreme Regional Court, Friesenplatz 12, Köln. And on the back he wrote his Paris address by hand, 5 *rue Lagrange, 5th Arrondisement*."

"A dump," she later called it, with a twinkle. Having been there myself, I can agree.

News of their meeting traveled fast among Margo's family. As Margo's brother Robert told me in 2012, "In 1933, my mother, her second husband Emil Netter and I went to Paris in Emil's Opel, stayed at Hotel Vernais, and visited our aunt. We heard there of the emergence of Paul Mayer in Margo's life, but had not yet met him."

***

Margarete Regina Charlotte Koch was quite the find. Margo, the familiar name for Margarete, was born in November 1912. She finished her schooling in Frankfurt and at the age of twenty "was sent" to Paris in the autumn of 1932 to study at the Sorbonne, as was not uncommon then for young women in families of her standing.

Margarete ("Margo") Regina Charlotte Koch, 1935

The elders in her family knew that formal study wasn't really her *forte*, but Margo was always an eager learner and was delighted to go, especially to Paris. Earlier that year, in the summer of 1932, she had lived in Croydon, a leafy suburb of South London, tending the home of a country parson and his wife, and working in the town's library. She loved it all, and found she loved being around books. When the Sorbonne didn't quite work out, she found employment in a bookstore near *l'Odeon,* also in the Latin Quarter.

After a lovely year in Paris, Margo heard of the new orders from Berlin seemingly aimed at her and decided to seek advice at Agency for Human Rights and met Paul. And went and had a drink with him. And discovered, though perhaps not immediately, that his place was a dump. A joyful Parisian romance ensued, the details of which were revealed later only with sly smiles. Suffice it to say, Paris was always their favorite city, and Margo was always his favorite woman. Paul was always smitten by his *Margaretechen*.

Not only was she beautiful, kind, resourceful and charming, she came from a family with a significant history and future.

***

Margo's mother, Ida Koch (née Kahn), was the beautiful and wealthy widow of Otto Koch, a man of high standing in Frankfurt on the Main River (*Frankfurt am Main*) that pours into the Rhine above Koblenz.

Before the Great War, Otto had been a great horseman who competed and excelled in *dressage* ("steeplechase") events all over Europe, and held a record for height that lasted several years. But once, when training for a competition, he was thrown by his horse and injured his shoulder. The injury nagged at him [sorry] throughout the War, and he promised himself and his young wife he'd get the necessary surgery as soon as war was over. He returned from the war a decorated cavalry officer (an officer in the Kaiser's cavalry was a huge rarity for a Jew), and went in for surgery. But despite then-common knowledge that dirty surgical instruments could be fatal, he died of blood poisoning just a few days afterwards, November 24, 1919.

Ida was bereft, and for a long time. Otto, the love of her life, died from a peacetime wound after finally returning from years of valorous service at the front. He died before he and she could even get properly re-connected, before Margo could really get to know him, and before his two very young sons could form any memory of him at all. A genuine tragedy.

Ida Kahn Koch, 1922, with Koch jewelry, as widow

Flashback: The source of Koch wealth is a story in itself requiring a book of its own. It entailed creation and ownership of one of the most significant jewelry stores in all Germany, indeed all Europe. It had its beginnings in 1879 in Baden-Baden in that town's heyday as *the* spa resort for European nobility after the influx of wealth from Prussia's victory over the French in 1870. Baden-Baden, still a beautiful small city, was famous the world over. Its spectacular casino is just like those used as a setting in James Bond movies.

This first store, begun by Otto's father Robert Koch, brilliantly illustrates the maxim "location, location, location." It was situated in the arcade just outside the *deluxe* casino, exactly where a gentleman emerges with a luscious lady on his arm following a good night at the tables. Brilliant, as were the diamonds and other jewels that made the store famous. And as I said, Baden-Baden was flush with money, both new and old.

A favorite family story: One day, important to the future line of Kochs and Mayers, the King of Siam visited Baden-Baden as part of his tour of Europe to learn what might be useful to his kingdom, like making Singha beer in the German manner. He entered the shop in the arcade by the casino, pointed with his cane to a significant portion of the highest end of Koch's inventory, and left. "What does all this cane-pointing mean?" the store manager asked the King's aide. He replied, "Those are the items he would like to buy."[9]

Presiding over two store upgrades in Frankfurt, Robert Koch Jeweler in 1883 was designated *Hofjuwelier* ("Jewelers to the Court," that is, the Court of the Emperor himself). Its store occupied the ground floor of a magnificent new Italianate building designed by the same architect as the famous *Reichstag* building in Berlin, at a magnificent location in Frankfurt, probably the best in the city. It thrived. Robert Koch himself died in 1902, passing leadership to his brother Louis. His son Otto became a partner.

One day (November 18, 1912) there was a bit of commotion at the store. Kaiser Wilhelm II's sister, Princess Charlotte, walked in, not for the first time, just as Otto was being toasted with champagne by the staff. When the Princess learned the cause of the merriment, that the owner is a proud first-time father, she insisted that infant

---

9   Many years later, I enacted a similar scene to return the favor. I was traveling in rural Siam (now Thailand) and came to a shop selling jeweled items made by local artisans. I pointed to a dozen choice items and doubled their asking price, thereby helping, I hope, to send one of their children to college.

Margarete carry her own name as one of her middle ones (Charlotte, not Regina as one might think).

Under the leadership of Robert's brother Louis Koch, the business developed a reputation comparable to Cartier of Paris or Tiffany of New York. Koch's tiaras adorned the crowned heads of Europe, and their beautifully designed hand-crafted jewelry was much in demand.[10]

By 1934, a few months after twenty-two year-old Margo met twenty-seven year-old Paul in Paris, they were in love. Margo changed jobs, leaving the bookstore which didn't sufficiently challenge her and found employment in March with *Librairie Ernest Flammarion*, a formidable bookstore and publisher then and now, then at 26 rue Racine where she worked until July 15, 1935.

And to think Paul had just fallen in love with an heiress to all this magnificence! Maybe as a lawyer he could become useful to the firm. The building still stands, quite unchanged, though without the jewelry store, as a neighbor of the hyper-modern Central Bank of Europe.

1935 – An oppressive year

Newsreel (1935)

March 16–Hitler violates the Treaty of Versailles by introducing military conscription.

September 15–German Jews stripped of rights by Nuremberg Race Laws. Jews can no longer be citizens or have the right to vote, according to the supplementary law enacted November 14.

---

10   Items crafted by the firm are still very much in demand, as any online search will reveal. A 1954 catalog commemorating the 75th anniversary of Robert Koch Jeweler can be found at https://frankfurter-personenlexikon.de/node/13694.

"Raus! You dirty Jews can no longer be German and no longer be citizens! Get out!"

Growing glory, that's what 1935 was to those who believed in the Nazi cause. To others not yet convinced of the 1933 handwriting on the wall, it was regarded as one more year of ever-ratcheting threats to their ability to survive life in Germany.

In 1935, new laws were enacted at a special meeting of the Reichstag convened during the annual week-long Nuremberg Rally of the Nazi Party, attended by over 700,000. By this time, the Nazis were masters at the high art of staging and filming over-the-top spectacles of massive crowds in massive arenas, with ritualized cult-like adoration of their leader, and torchlight parades of tens of thousands stomping in jackboots into the night.

During this year's Party rally, new "Nuremberg Laws" were designed to accelerate the exclusion of Jews (and others) from German society. By law, German Jews were no longer "German Jews." They were declared "Jews in Germany," a phrase creating a pretext for exclusion and expulsion.

There were two key laws. The first was bravely named the *"Law for the Protection of German Blood and German Honor."* It forbade marriage and any intimate extramarital relations between Jews and non-Jewish German citizens (the latter denigrated as "race disgrace").

The second was the *"Reich Citizenship Law,"* which declared that only those of German blood (defined after several months of drafting and re-drafting as having no more than one Jewish grandparent) or Aryan (an Aryan being a person with blond hair and blue eyes of Germanic heritage) were eligible to be Reich citizens. The remainder were classed as state subjects without any citizenship rights. On November 14, Jews could no longer be citizens or have the right to vote.[11] The laws were expanded on November 26 declar-

---

11 Friedländer, Saul (2009). *Nazi Germany and the Jews, 1933–1945.*

ing "Romani (known then as Gypsies), and Black people, and Jews as enemies of the race-based state."

"*Raus!* A marriage won't save you! Get out!"

"The word "marriage" never crossed our lips," Margo said later, "but we knew it would happen."

Paul the disbarred German lawyer gathered documents to support application for travel visas to the United States to explore the possibility of life there, if it ever came to that. They had never been there and didn't know anyone, but solicited the support of a distant relative on the Koch side, Fanny Abraham, wife of Simon Abraham, "a prominent merchant and capitalist in Louisiana," as stated in their application.

In May, Paul received a signed Affidavit of Support, which claimed "the undermentioned alien (Paul Mayer) desires to come to the US because of political conditions in Germany which make it unbearable for Jews to live there." In August, Paul was granted a Quota Immigration Visa by US Dept of State in Stuttgart, set to expire 14 December 1935, four months later.

This cleared the way for Paul to travel to the US. Why Paul would get a visa and not Margo is a mystery, but presumably if he and Margo were married, they could both go. But they didn't go.[12]

Instead, Paul accepted work in Köln at M. Lissauer & Company, the minerals and alloys processing company where he'd earlier served in Fall 1929 as a beginning law student. This option was made more attractive by the fact that Lissauer, a Jewish-owned enterprise, also had an office in Amsterdam, which could be useful just in case. In fact, one of the partners of the firm told Paul, "If trouble ever comes, we'll transfer you to our Amsterdam office." This indeed sounded hopeful.

New York: HarperCollins. ISBN 978-0-06-1350276.

12   The original Application for Immigration Visa, the Visa itself, and Immigrant Identification Card are in the Archives, and they look entirely unused.

Margo remained in Paris working for Flammarion until July, when she returned to Frankfurt, and then spent a lovely summer in Venice with her two brothers and very likely also her mother with her new husband, Emil Netter.

Otto Erich, Margo, and Robert showing off in Venice, summer 1935

At this point, in August 1935, Paul still thought he and Margo would be able to live the kinds of lives God intended for them, in Germany. Paul still thought the troubles would pass, that his compatriots' fascination with the Nazis would pass. One big reason to support this: there had already been a few attempts on Hitler's life. But evidently, Lissauer's assurance that it would look after him was what Paul needed to hear, since, evidently, he let his Quota Immigration Visa lapse, unused.

Newsreel (1936)

February 10—The German Gestapo (Secret Service) is placed above the law.

May 9—Mussolini's Italian forces take Ethiopia.

July 18—Civil war erupts in Spain.

August 1—Olympic games begin in Berlin.

Celebration and hope

Paul and Margarete Regina Charlotte Koch were married in the Westend Synagogue in Frankfurt-am-Main on May 26, 1936, at an event that was most likely joyful and tense at the same time.

Paul and Margo's wedding day, Frankfurt, May 26, 1936

This photo shows the distinguished families of Koch and Kahn, Margo's father and mother, who came to the wedding fully welcoming. In addition to Margo (back center), we see (top left) her younger brothers Robert (born 1918) and Erich Otto (born 1919), at that time preparing for lives in the Koch Jeweler business in capacities not yet spelled out. Also present, Margo's young Kahn cousins, Hans, Peter, Eva, and Wolf (very front), at the time imagining themselves as artists and musicians. These beautiful kids were all staying at their grandmother Anna Kahn's home nearby in Frankfurt's West End while their father, Emil Kahn (Ida's brother) prepared the future for them in New York.[13]

Who stands out in this wedding photo? Not exactly mugging for the camera, there's Paul, the sober and serious one. Was he glad to be there? Let's hope so, though with his old-fashioned, decorous pose for this photo it's not easy to tell.

He is the oldest, and therefore, per custom, the most decorous, of this newly merged Mayer/Koch/Kahn clan by at least five years. He is the one most rooted in the pre-Great War generation, the Kaiser's generation, the pre-Weimar generation. His generation has been much more influenced by those features of the past than his new kin, who are all thoroughgoing "Weimar babies." These youngsters were educated in Weimar schools that emphasize more contemporary democratic and humanistic values even more than Paul's more classical education in Catholic, Prussian, Imperial Köln.

His new Koch kin were educated in Frankfurt's Goethe Gymnasium and were eager intellectual entrepreneurs ready to participate in the life of the family's jewelry business. And his new Kahn kin were more adventurous and of experimental artistic temperament, much less rooted to the Old-World order.

While the marriage ceremony was conducted at Frankfurt's Westend Synagogue, it was then celebrated at the Frankfurter Hof, the best hotel in this proudly democratically spirited city, the same

---

13 For a fascinating account of life in this storied period of near idyllic life in beautiful progressive Frankfurt between the wars, see Sylvia Tennenbaum, *Yesterday's Streets*, New York: Random House, 1981.

hotel where Margo's own parents, Otto Koch and Ida Kahn, had celebrated their wedding soon after the hotel was built in 1911. It's also where Susan and I privately celebrated our just legalized marriage at the end of 2016 on our way to Amsterdam.

It's interesting that no photos exist of any of the Mayer family at the wedding—no Mayers and no Teutschs, though Paul's father and mother were certainly there, and there may have been some local Teutschs as well. A tremendous gift from the Teutsch family was presented to Paul and Margo, a magnificently constructed and handsomely printed *Stammbaum* ("family tree") covering the Teutsch family of Venningen since 1590. Created by Albert Teutsch (a second cousin of Paul's), it took many large pages to show all the different branches of the tree. Two printed versions somehow survived.

There was to be no honeymoon yet.

"*Raus!* Are you deaf? You can run but you can't hide! Get out!"

Paul and Margo pretended life was normal, as normal as it could be in Nazified Germany with all its limitations. But while they may have taken up married life expecting normal life, life was not normal. They may have found it tolerable, but it was certainly not normal.

As was the custom, they took up residence in the husband's city, Köln, at Kleingedankstrasse 16, a thirty-minute walk from Paul's parents' home at Friesenplatz 12. They began a life of what could be called "lobstering," where the lobster (or frog, in less privileged settings) in the cooking pot barely notices the cooking water heating up from a slow simmer until …until it's too late to escape the killing boil. One might wonder why anyone would stay after noticing the pain, but thousands of stories will attest to the difficulty of picking up and moving far from harm's way, especially if it means moving one's family, history, and future.

Is it too painful yet? Everyone has their own threshold of pain. But the rhetorical question surely went out, "Will someone please turn down the heat?!" With hindsight it's easy to see the progression to its still unknown end, but obviously in real time, no one can know what tomorrow will bring. Paul and Margo were still optimistic, and they were not alone, that a major intervention in this progression would naturally or magically or inevitably take place. Hitler was not universally loved and, as I said, no one knows what people will do or what new possibilities take shape.

German Jews who were still there in 1936 later reported how they constantly gauged the water temperature as well as their own tolerance and chances of survival. In one seemingly trivial but long-remembered instance related years later, Margo and Paul felt compelled to sneak out of their home in the middle of the night to a nearby park where they furtively disposed of a letter opener under some bushes as far away from the streetlamp as possible. An order had gone out prohibiting Jews from carrying "bladed instruments or weapons," which caused Margo and Paul to take inventory. They were always scrupulously compliant, as they were both German, after all, and an official regulation is an official regulation.

They worried that their letter opener looked enough like a dagger to be taken for one of those recently banned "bladed instrument or weapon." Amusing, perhaps, but what does it say when you lose the dignity of walking freely at night, with or without a letter opener, for fear of being frisked? No one carried guns at that time, not Jews and not other Germans, it just wasn't part of the culture. But fear of being frisked for a letter opener? By an officer of Nazi law?

Paul, with Margo steadfast at his side, was still committed to staying but decided to keep his options open and stay above board. He maintained his official relationship with the authorities. On August 15, 1936, he wrote to the American Consulate, "to keep the record straight, I haven't used the Visa issued August 5, 1935. The reason is that I have not yet lost my job as I feared last year."

***

The cooking water continued to simmer. Paul and Margo, probably at Margo's instigation, again allowed themselves the thought of maybe possibly picking up and moving to the United States. I say this with obvious frustration–what's taking you so long?–but for Margo and especially Paul, it was still, if I haven't made this point clear enough, a difficult decision to make. To pick up and move one's entire life to another place across the ocean, leaving behind whatever dreams they still entertained for a life together in Germany? Yes, people do it all the time, but it's typically an act of desperation when staying is finally deemed impossible.

The United States was *terra incognita* for most European Jews. As the noted historian Walter Laqueur explained in his book, *Generation Exodus*, "Most Germans in the 1930s had a general idea what life was like in the neighboring European countries but knew very little about America except some stereotypes: cowboys and Indians and the tremendously popular books of Karl May with the nineteenth-century Wild West as a background, the skyscrapers, Hollywood (including jazz and the gangster movies), chewing gum, big cars, and cheap products sold in certain chain stores."[14]

Paul himself shared this image of America, from Karl May to chewing gum, and was skeptical about a future there. But he relented and chose to go with Margo and his sister Illa to see for themselves.

In May 1937, Margo was issued a passport enabling her to leave the country, valid until December 31, 1938. And on June 11, Paul, Margo, and Illa set sail from Southampton on the SS President Harding to New York. I have the passenger list.

---

14 Walter Laqueur, *Generation Exodus: The Fate of Young Jewish Refugees From Nazi Germany,* Brandeis University Press, 2001.

Margo aboard the SS President Harding, May 1937.

They travelled the eastern seaboard by train from New York to New Orleans, visiting a few friends and Margo's Louisiana relations along the way. When done, Paul decided, sure enough, there's no possibility of life there–"too many Americans."

Yes, Paul was a snob, and even with all the conditions they were forced to endure in Germany, Paul determined that they could safely stay in Germany with him employed at Lissauer, and that the growing storm would all blow over. We'll hear this again and again...

He really *wanted* to stay, it's safe to say. He really did *not* want to leave. His roots there went deep, and he felt committed. Commitment is admirable, one can say, but commitment to what? The reader can guess as well as I can. Even so, can there be no end to this commitment? When, finally, can one give oneself permission to go? Not yet, apparently. Paul was resolved, and Margo was flexible.

1938 – The worst year possible

Newsreel (first half 1938)

March—Nazi troops enter Austria, which has a population of 200,000 Jews, mainly living in Vienna. Hitler announces Anschluss (union) with Austria. After the Anschluss, the Secret Service (Gestapo) is placed in charge of Jewish affairs in Austria with Adolf Eichmann establishing an Office for Jewish Emigration in Vienna. Himmler establishes Mauthausen concentration camp near Linz.

April and June—Nazis order Jews to register wealth and property. Nazis order Jewish-owned businesses to register.

In the written memoirs of survivors, 1938 is sometimes called *annus horribilis* ("the horrible year"—a counter to *annus mirabilis*—"the wondrous year" of John Keats, the Romantic poet). It was certainly a dreadful, eventful year for Paul and Margo, and for anyone and everyone in the crosshairs of the Nazi policies.

The Nuremberg Laws of 1935 had a crippling economic and social impact on the Jewish community. Persons convicted of violating the marriage laws were imprisoned, and (subsequent to March 1938) upon completing their sentences were re-arrested by the Gestapo and sent to Nazi concentration camps. (Concentration camps were not yet purposed as extermination camps, which came later, in 1941). Non-Jews gradually stopped socializing with Jews or shopping in Jewish-owned stores, many of which closed due to a lack of customers.

As Jews were no longer permitted to work in the civil service or government-regulated professions such as medicine and education, many middle-class business owners and professionals were forced to take menial employment. Emigration was problematic, as Jews were required to remit up to ninety percent of their wealth as a tax upon leaving the country. By 1938 it was almost impossible for Jews wanting to emigrate to find a country willing to take them. Mass deportation schemes such as the Madagascar Plan proved to be impossible for the Nazis to carry out. Those wanting to leave were virtually trapped.

The lobsterpot got ever hotter. The Nazis kept adding to the heavy timbers of the Nuremberg Laws with additional wood, adding restrictions to induce the stubborn to jump the pot and flee. There was something new every day, it seemed. Jews were now forbidden from owning private gardens. All streets in Germany needed to be renamed, erasing memories and associations except those blessed by Nazi ideology. Jews were forbidden from attending movie theaters, the opera, and concerts. Jewish children were barred from attending public school.[15]

Simply put, the fucking Nazis were masters at trivializing and dehumanizing the lives of those they targeted. Almost everything that one could do, have, or be *before* Hitler took over, could now not be done, with severe penalties for non-compliance. People were scared, and increasingly, so were the other nations and governments of Europe and their colonial descendants.

Mass uncertainty prevailed, at least among the officially unwanted. No one knew where they'd be at the end of the year, or what would come after that. By this time, the gates were closing around the world. Savings were being depleted as extortionist bureaucrats and border officials thrived.

---

15   Peter Longerich, *Holocaust: The Nazi Persecution and Murder of the Jews*. Oxford; New York: Oxford University Press, 2010.

***

This was also the time when Margo experienced her first pregnancy. She and Paul were very much in love and saw a family as their rightful future. Another effing opportunity to weigh their options. Could this be an opportunity to start that family, in defiance of all the obstacles? And if not, could they access the now-hostile health system to terminate the pregnancy? What a terrible position to be in. Either choice would be anguishing.

Through the rising mist from the simmering lobster pot, they divine that while perhaps they themselves could stay in Germany, it was not a good time to raise a child. Fortunately, Paul's father was still connected to other doctors. The procedure was performed illegally out of the sight of disapproving eyes, and the instruments were clean.

But the pain of that memory lingered. It took many more years, a dreadfully long time, through flight, poverty, and war, before they felt safe and secure enough to allow themselves to begin a family. Years later, when she was thirty-three, at a time of personal security, one of the first charities Margo gave money to was Planned Parenthood of America.

***

"We can't keep on like this," Margo told Paul. And Paul too *finally* began to recognize the situation as dire. And when Paul recognizes a situation as dire, he writes about it. He began recording the events of the day in earnest, in a small pocket journal or daybook. He also began collecting the documents a lawyer might find useful for quick emigration, keeping a good paper trail for the future.

"Let's see what Amsterdam is like." On February 25, Paul and Margo took the train to Amsterdam to reconnoiter, to imagine life there. While in Köln, they'd begun Dutch lessons. And so far, it seemed that Lissauer & Co. had every intention of honoring its promise to Paul: "If trouble ever comes, we can move you to our Amsterdam office." That promise from Lissauer was certainly an essential element figuring into Paul's decision to wait it out in Germany. If worst came to worse, they could slip across the nearby border and cross into Holland, to Amsterdam, where they would, they assumed, be out of reach of the Nazi Government of Germany.

At breakfast at the Café Port van Cleve, as recounted in my introduction to this book, they try to answer the question, "This seems like a nice enough place. Do we pull up stakes and move here, or do we take the train back and stay in Germany until this blows over?"

Anyone watching this movie yells, "Are you kidding me?! You must go! Go! Get out while you can!"

"Don't yell at us," is their response, "You don't know how this will turn out any more than we do."

They had been living comfortably, all things considered, at their home at Kleingedankstrasse 16, since the wedding two years earlier. Paul loved the city and being near his parents. For Margo, it was a new city, and an entirely new role as a live-at-home wife and as a daughter-in-law. She knew how to do family, and felt close to her in-laws. Paul went to work every day at Lissauer, where he could no longer represent clients in court but he could still work as an office lawyer. do As a whole they "adapted to circumstances," to use Margo's phrase decades later. When Margo's younger brother, nineteen-year-old Erich Otto, came to visit them at their Köln home in March while a new student at Cambridge University, he remarked to me years later, "they seemed quite content."

If Paul and Margo left Köln bound for *anywhere*, they would be leaving behind Paul's parents Ernst and ELisbeth, and Margo's mother Ida Kahn and Ida's mother Anna S. Kahn, both living in Frankfurt. Could they?

Could they leave Paul's parents behind? Ernst was conducting a very limited medical practice under severe restrictions. He too had no wish to get up and leave. "My patients need me here," he told the Gestapo when they arrived at his door to take him in. "I have surgery scheduled this afternoon." The Gestapo saw fit to leave, that time.

Could they move to Frankfurt to be near Margo's mother and grandmother? Ida Kahn was living alone there, having been widowed twice (Emil Netter died just before Margo's wedding) but still had partnership responsibilities in Robert Koch Jewelers. Her mother Anna S. Kahn also remained in Frankfurt. Anna had lost a husband and a son in the Great War, and her remaining son Emil Kahn, who had been dismissed from service as conductor of the Stuttgart Symphony Orchestra, had earlier decamped to the US.

By their calculation, there was still reason to stay, and that's what they decided to do. Whether they were paralyzed and frozen in place, or in complete denial of the threat virtually everyone else felt, or lulled by their general contentment, or were resolutely defiant ("No one can tell us we don't deserve to be here!") is hard to say, and those are four *very* different states of mind.

***

Not everyone dithered. Illa and her new husband Dr. Gottlieb Marum, who were married in March of that year, decided to leave.

Illa had tried also to have a career of her own but it was her mother and not the Nazis that prevented that. Inspired perhaps by her experiences in her father's doctor's office, as well as with the family dogs, and most certainly with the wild boar corralled at the family's hunting cabin in the Eifel, Illa wanted to become a veterinarian doctor. Unfortunately, her mother deemed it "not suitable," and that was apparently the last word. Lisbeth's word, at least on the subject of a career for Illa, carried weight. Illa, a woman of few words, admitted she always resented the role her mother played in directing her life.

There are photos from their honeymoon, taken from their hotel window in Vienna, of Austrian Nazi troopers marching directly below. Years later Illa told me how ominous it felt, those troops with jackboots menacing on the cobbled street, and the motorcade of Nazi leadership, and how she easily could have dropped a flowerpot directly on Mr. Hitler's *kopf*. She forever regretted that she hadn't.

Gottlieb was perfect for her—German, Jewish, and a Doctor of Medicine specializing in radiology, just like her father. Unlike Paul, Gottlieb believed the writing he saw on the wall. "There's a better future for us in America than here," they had concluded. Illa presumably felt as close to her parents as Paul did; when Gottlieb secured a position in Wheeling, West Virginia, she probably felt relieved by Paul's strong wish to stay in Köln with their parents. But it was surely a poignant moment when in June, Paul wrote in his daybook, "Our last evening on *Neumarkt* [the Marum family home.]"

The next day Paul took Illa and Gottlieb to the train station in Köln to begin their journey to the New World. Illa and Gottlieb were still allowed to ship ahead all the gifts of their wedding ceremony, including beautiful Bauhaus furniture, silverware and table settings for twelve. Such permission for émigrés was denied shortly after.

Auf wiedersehen, mein leib bruder! Auf wiedersehen, meine leibe schwester!

While on shipboard crossing the Atlantic, Gottlieb received a telegram stating that the position offered by the Wheeling Clinic was withdrawn. Apparently the West Virginia State legislature decided not to permit any more German Jewish doctors, despite the reputation of German doctors, especially radiologists, as being among the best on the planet. Fortunately, the state of Mississippi had not seen fit to exclude German Jewish doctors, as it greatly needed *any* doctors, and Gottlieb was offered a similar position in Greenville, Mississippi. Their truckload of furnishings first went to Wheeling and finally caught up with them in Greenville, a small southern city known for its rich literary history and a significant Jewish presence[16] that they grew very fond of.[17]

Illa and Dr. Gottlieb Marum, 1943

***

---

16   "Oh, you mean Jew-town?" asked the ticket taker at the train station in New Orleans.

17   Their newspaper, the *Delta Democrat-Times* (published by Pulitzer Prize winner Hodding Carter), was delivered to the Marums daily by a Theartrice ("T") Williams, a young boy at the time before becoming a civil rights activist in Minneapolis, with critical positions at Phyllis Wheatley Community Center, The Urban Coalition, Minnesota Department of Corrections, Hubert Humphrey Center for Public Affairs, before serving with distinction as Senior Associate with my nonprofit consulting organization, Rainbow Research, Inc. "T" and I learned this remarkable coincidence while traveling in the South together while working on a grant from the Ford Foundation on "Community Philanthropy and Racial Equity in the American South."

Two days after Illa and Gottlieb departed for West Virginia, Paul and Margo decided to re-open the door to the America option, despite there being too many Americans there, and to begin again the quest for a US visa.

On June 23, Margo took up pen again and wrote to her distant relative in New Orleans, where her brother Robert was already residing.

"Dear Mamere *(Abraham)*, Margo writes in impeccable English. "You have probably heard ... that things have grown worse for us in this country...The general depression amongst our co-religionnaires is increasing, and for the first time our personal outlook must be regarded as hopeless since, caused by the present situation, Paul's career in his business-firm is no more assured. Although he is still keeping his job there, he might lose it in the course of this year, as the days of Jewish firms seems to be counted. We therefore have made up our minds to leave this country as soon as possible, and as you have always so very kindly offered your help..."

One can imagine this was a difficult letter to write, after all they'd been through. They were clearly throwing in the towel.

"Raus! We'll make it impossible for you filthy Jews to stay!"

Newsreel (late 1938)

July—At Evian, France, the U.S. convenes a League of Nations conference with delegates from thirty-two countries to consider helping Jews fleeing Hitler, but no country will accept them.

July—Nazis prohibit Jews from providing a variety of specified commercial services. Nazis prohibit Jewish doctors from all practice of medicine.

August 12—German military mobilizes for war.

August 17—Nazis require Jewish women to add "Sara" and men to add "Israel" to their names on all legal documents including passports.

September 27—Nazis prohibit Jews from all legal practices.

Still determined to stay in his Germany, Paul reported in his 1938 daybook a series of events finally seeking help from the US government that would allow him and Margo to leave Germany. The US is of no help.

On July 7, Paul receives a sworn affidavit from their relatives in Louisiana, "Mrs. Simon Abraham born Fanny Schwartz, 1512 Seventh Street, New Orleans, born in New Orleans, wife of Simon Abraham, merchant of Raceland, Louisiana, member of the Board of the Bank of Raceland, owners of large merchandise store in Raceland in support of Mr. and Mrs. Paul Mayer (Cologne), desiring of entering the US as quota immigrants."

On July 20, Paul writes to the US Foreign Service in Stuttgart asking for official permission to enter the US. In the letter he reminds the Consular Service that "on August 16, 1935, you were kind enough to grant me Quota-Immigration Visa 20124, which I had the regret of being unavoidably prevented from making use of."

On August 3, Paul receives a letter from the American Consul in Stuttgart: "You are informed that in order to establish your priority for an immigration visa, it will be necessary for you to apply for registration on the waiting list of intending immigrants, and it is suggested that you fill out and return the enclosed form. Since your turn on the waiting list would not be reached before next year, it is not practicable to examine at this time the documents.."

On August 18, Paul, new to the family but acting as a lawyer, is invited by Margo's Onkel Ludwig Heilbrunn, a partner in the Robert Koch Jewelers, to sit in on a meeting with the huge German company, Robert Bosch and Co., to discuss "Aryanization" of Koch Jewelers. Jewish-owned businesses were under great duress, essentially being forced to sell to "Aryans." A deal was made for Bosch to buy Koch Jewelers at fire sale prices, though Bosch was later said to have "behaved well" in this transaction, and Koch Jewelers kept its name throughout the Nazi era, one of the very few Jewish-owned stores with this distinction, and even beyond Bosch's ownership until the store's eventual closing in 1987, more than one hundred years after its founding

On September 6 they receive an affidavit sworn in New Orleans by Robert Bernhard Max Koch (Margo's brother), that Paul and Margo "will never become public charges or depend upon charity in any form."

But the affidavit is too late. The decision by the American Consul in Stuttgart just weeks earlier to put Paul and Margo at the end of the line is discouraging, to say the least.

It's the end of this road, it would seem. Opportunities denied, denied, denied.

Not only can't they go to America, they no longer have the lifeline to Amsterdam they were counting on. Paul's employment at Lissauer & Co. was jerked away by the same Nazi policy of Aryanization of Jewish-owned business that led to the loss of the Koch family business. Lissauer was sold to Aryans.

While Lissauer had promised to send Paul to Amsterdam "if trouble ever comes," its new Aryan owner had no interest in honoring the promise. Paul and Margo were now stranded in Köln with no lifeline.

One can only wonder what would have happened to Paul and Margo if they had taken up life in Amsterdam. Years later, while touring the Anne Frank house in Amsterdam with my mother and brother, Margo said more than once, "It could have been us. The Frank's fate would have been ours too."

Ernst and Lisbeth, at home in Köln acting normally

Newsreel (late 1938)

October 5–New law requires Jewish passports to be stamped with a large red "J."

October 15–28–German troops move into the Sudetenland; Czech government resigns. Nazis arrest 17,000 Jews of Polish nationality living in Germany, deporting them to Poland, which refuses them entry, leaving them in 'No-Man's Land' near the Polish border for several months.

November 9–10–*Kristallnacht* ("The Night of Broken Glass")—For Paul and Margo, the final straw.

"*Raus*! We'll burn you out! Get out! Good riddance!"

Days followed days, and on October 1, two important things happened. Paul departed Lissauer, which at least wrote a decent reference, but that's it. "He left our services for the well-known reasons…" Yes, a very decent reference, one can say sarcastically. Paul ended the day seeking help from the American Consulate in Köln.

"Denied."

There are no more entries for the rest of October in Paul's daybook. One can imagine him increasingly depressed, perhaps even questioning his determination to stay. Months earlier, he was at least free to leave Germany. They could have chosen to stay in Amsterdam, working for Lissauer and living a new life with Margo in one of those fine canal houses while the Nazis pursued their cruel Thousand Year agenda just up the River, but the sale of Lissauer would have stranded them in Amsterdam with no employment and no apparent prospects at all. By October, even the Netherlands closed its borders to Jews. And as Margo noted later, "We could have been with the Franks."

Staying in Germany was by then without further prospects. Paul had lost his job and their escape route to Amsterdam. Permission to go to the US was denied. Margo's family's business, worth a substantial fortune just a few years earlier, was now savaged in a forced sale to "Aryan" business interests. His right to practice law had been stripped. His father's right to practice medicine had been stripped and their home sold out from under them. His sister and her new husband, Margo's brothers and cousins—all had fled.

Paul and Margo hunkered down deeper, held in place by mysterious forces, a combination of duty, bewilderment, helplessness, impossibility, and defiance. Apparently the pressure to leave was not yet sufficiently felt, the case to leave not yet sufficiently clear. They kept on.

***

October came and went.

In November, a crisis opened a way out in ways they could never have imagined. This was a crisis that Nazi leadership created to induce riotous action that would chase out the few Jews remaining.

In two days of frightening chaos and destruction *Kristallnacht*, (November 9-10, "The night of broken glass") named from the shards that littered the streets after the windows of Jewish-owned stores were smashed by paramilitary forces and civilians, Jewish homes, hospitals, schools, and synagogues were ransacked as attackers demolished buildings with sledgehammers. Rioters destroyed over 1,400 synagogues and prayer rooms throughout Germany, Austria, and the Sudetenland. Over 7,000 Jewish businesses were damaged or destroyed, and 30,000 Jewish men were arrested and incarcerated in concentration camps.[18]

In his 1938 Daybook, Paul wrote in practiced but terse English that almost captures his rising apprehension:

> "November 7, I heard at the radio that a seventeen-year-old German-born Polish Jew living in Paris had shot and wounded Mr. Ernst von Rath, Secretary at the German Embassy in Paris.
>
> Two nights later Margo and I happened to be hosting new friends Mr. and Mrs. A.J. Fallowfield, the British Consul General in Köln. They came for dinner and a game of bridge. With the radio on, we all heard that Mr. von Rath had just died. We sensed trouble, and staying

---

18 British historian Martin Gilbert wrote that no event in the history of German Jews between 1933 and 1945 was so widely reported as it was happening, and the accounts from foreign journalists working in Germany drew worldwide attention. *The Times* of London observed on 11 November 1938: "No foreign propagandist bent upon blackening Germany before the world could outdo the tale of burnings and beatings, of blackguardly assaults on defenceless and innocent people, which disgraced that country yesterday." www.Wikipedia.com/Krystallnacht.

up past midnight, we listened to the British Broadcasting Corporation's coverage of events, including British Prime Minister Mr. Neville Chamberlain's speech at the London Guild Hall.

Call on me if I can be of help, Mr. Fallowfield said as they departed.

The next day, November 10, Papa & Mama came to our home and rushed in, telling that the police were rounding up Jews, smashing store windows, burning synagogues, etc. They told us to take the car and drive to Frankfurt, since their Köln address was registered with the police, and we could easily be rounded up. We saw demonstrations on the road, and turned on to back roads. We made it to Frankfurt and hid in [Ida's] attic.

A few days later, when it felt a bit safer, we set out for Köln late in the evening. On the way, in the Taunus hills [southwest of Frankfurt], we suffered a flat tire. I couldn't change it, but we could see the lights of a tavern down the road, and I suggested Margo could persuade someone to come and help. She went ahead and returned with an eager young man while I stayed at the car, waiting. Fortunately, the tire was changed with no further incident."

Scared—that's the feeling one can almost get from Paul's entries, the feeling of Fear. Nothing evokes it like the sight of fire approaching and men screaming for blood.

The events of Kristallnacht allowed Paul finally to hear-and to heed-his parents' encouragement to leave, to take care of their own future somewhere else, out of Germany. His focus shifted to survival. He and Margo reached for an opportunity offered them just days earlier by the British Consul in Köln, whom they'd met only a few weeks earlier at a social function, and even had to their home for dinner and bridge. The Consul had offered his assistance if it were needed; Paul allowed as how that time had come, and sought a meeting with him.

"Go to America," Mr. Fallowfield told Paul and Margo on November 14, "but not from here. You should know that America's door isn't exactly open anymore to Jews from Germany. We believe it's possible you can get a visa to travel from here to Britain, a transit visa that lets you stay for one year. You can't earn wages, but you can apply for an entry visa from there to America. We understand the US State Department is more amenable to that arrangement."

So now, the door had opened. There was a good chance of going to the US after a year in England, where at least they'd be safe. It's as good an arrangement as any, it would seem, and anything could still happen in a year's time. Fallowfield had given them the best advice possible, and showed them a way out.

They filled out some paperwork, and the Brits responded affirmatively. On November 25th, with the proper British papers in hand, Paul recorded their formal application for passports at the police station in Köln.

"Not so fast, *Juden*," they said once again. "First you have pay for all the damage you caused on Kristallnacht. You have to pay for the cleanup, and a fine for our troubles." This bill, levied throughout Germany, was enormous. There was also a Refugee Tax for those fortunate enough to secure legal flight from Germany at this late date, also enormous. In 2025 US dollars, it was the equivalent of 650,000 dollars for the Refugee Tax, and 470,000 dollars for Kristallnacht damages.

"OK, OK..."

"Everyone's telling us it's time to go. We seem to have run out of options," Paul said to no one in particular. It turns out he was right about running out of options. I know of only one person who stayed longer and made it out alive.

Also at this time, Ernst and Lisbeth were forced to sell their substantial home at Friesenplatz 12, their home of long-standing. Because it was also his place of practice, with labs and workrooms for constructing prosthesis, it was large enough to attract the industrial giant Siemens which purchased it for a song. Ernst and Lisbeth now had to move to a smaller apartment.

On December 19, Paul and Margo were somehow able to pay the extortionate fines the Nazis levied on them to clean up the country after Kristallnacht, and gave permission to Paul and Margo to leave. On December 21, they issued passports to both Paul and Margo. On December 23, the police provided them with "Good Conduct Certificates." It was the least they could do.

Now came the hard part, requiring the two bravest steps they hadn't yet taken: they actually had to leave, but first they actually had to say goodbye. That list included Paul's parents, his mother's mother Emma living in Köln, and Margo's grandmother Anna, a bereft widow of many years rattling around alone in her big home in the West End. Margo's mother Ida was still there, though she intended to go to London as soon as the sale of Koch Jewelers permitted. They were leaving not only these elders but their comfortable homes in Köln and Frankfurt as well as their little lobster apartment and their almost perfect lives in their almost perfect land where they'd happily grown up.

And if it's possible actually to leave one's future behind, they left that too.

On December 27, 1938 they said their good-byes, which words and my imagination to describe these scenes fail me, and with two suitcases, a typewriter, the clothes on their backs and no silver or table settings, they started off to the airport. And then, of course, the plan went awry. Their plane was grounded because of snowy weather, and they had to change plans at the very last minute.

Usually, when trying to leave a place one is ready to leave, there's increasing tension that something might go wrong as the time draws closer. In this case, with as much anticipation as this had, the tension must have been unbearable. But bear it they did. They hired a private car from their home to meet his parents at the Dom Hotel, walked together to the train station next door, and boarded a train to Rotterdam.

"*Auf wiedersehen, mein liebes kind*," Ernst and Lisbeth wave as their train pulls out. "Good-bye, my beloved children."

From Hoek van Holland, the passenger port next to Rotterdam, they took the overnight boat to Harwich, England, about eight hours across the Channel, and then the train to Liverpool Street Station in central London, to begin their lives in exile.

"...and fuck you!"

The day after arriving in England, Paul thumbed his nose at the fucking Nazis in an unusual expression of defiance. In a note to the police in Köln, he wrote, "Pursuant to the regulations of August 1938 regarding change of first and last names, I hereby inform you that as of January 1, 1939, I am dropping 'Israel' and 'Margaret' is dropping 'Sarah.'"

That must have felt at least a little bit satisfying.

They celebrated New Year's Eve at a wonderful affair to which they'd been escorted by Otto Erich Koch, Margo's rather dashing and eager Cambridge University student brother with social connections, connections which were supposed to have been major assets to the Koch Jewelers firm in the world that the lovely Weimar years had predicted for him, the world now practically disintegrated.[19]

---

19 Described wonderfully in Eric Koch, *I Remember The Location Exactly*, Mosaic Press, 2010

Book 2: War

With a fine hangover, Paul and Margo landed soberly in their small, rented room in Kensington just three days after arriving in London. They began the year adrift between two worlds: between Germany and the US, between the past and the future, between peace and war, and who knows what?

Newsreel (1939)

August 23–Nazis and Soviets sign a Non-Aggression Pact.

August 31–British fleet mobilizes; civilian evacuations begin from London.

September 1–Nazis invade Poland.

September 3–Britain, France, Australia and New Zealand declare war on Germany.

September 5–United States proclaims its neutrality.

September 10–Canada declares war on Germany; Battle of the Atlantic begins.

September 29–Nazis and Soviets divide up Poland.

October–Nazis begin euthanasia on sick and disabled in Germany.

"Warning to Brits! The Krauts are coming!"

In the early light of 1939 Paul contemplated the future and feared the worst. Not so much for himself and his wife, but more for the world, and most immediately for England and Great Britain. Paul and Margo liked England, Margo very much so from memories of her idyllic summer there a few years earlier, and Paul by temperament. But Britain, Paul knew, even if the Brits did not, was under imminent threat.

Throughout the year, Paul wrote many urgent letters to Official Britain, warning them of impending disaster, imploring them to take heed. "The Krauts are coming! The Krauts are coming!" Paul offered his help as an economist/lawyer who understands the German mind.

He threw himself into warning them and offering his expertise, with solid introductory letters to many governmental and non-governmental agencies: The Department of Overseas Trade, The Home Office, The Ministry of Supply, The Board of Trade, Cotton Spinners and Manufacturers, Northeastern Railways, Department of Overseas Trade, BBC, Ministry of Supply, Air Ministry, British Metals Corporation, Ministry of Economic Warfare, Ministry of Labor, and War Office.

Sometimes there was no response, and sometimes there was an official acknowledgment. But in the end there would come an official British rebuff to the effect, "Why should we trust you? You're a German too!"

Paul wrote to his brother-in-law Erich Otto Koch at Cambridge, "The Germans are ever so much better at war preparation than the Brits."

Paul received a letter from his former girlfriend from Köln, the one before Margo, who wrote plaintively to him. "Will I ever see you again?" Paul kept the letter, as did Margo. "Killed in Auschwitz," Margo wrote on its archived folder.

Newsreel (1939)

September 1–Nazis invade Poland.

September 3–Britain, France, Australia and New Zealand declare war on Germany.

September 5–United States proclaims its neutrality

September 10–Canada declares war on Germany, but US proclaims its neutrality; Battle of the Atlantic begins.

September 29–Nazis and Soviets divide up Poland.

October–Nazis begin euthanasia on sick and disabled in Germany.

A disjointed life

From London, Paul and Margo read the above news of an impending war becoming increasingly obvious as 1939 wore on. They were required to live a disjointed life, both physically and emotionally. They couldn't put down roots in England, so they couldn't be at home there, or in Germany, or the US. They knew that their transit visa permitted them only one year. England was only a place for further transition. The clock was always ticking down. They waited amidst dread and uncertainty.

They moved into larger quarters and carried on a domestic life which they shared with Margo's mother Ida, who had arrived soon after they had. They lived at least partly on the proceeds of sales of antique clocks and watches, part of Margo's father's collection that arrived from Frankfurt through mysterious channels, presumably helped by Koch store employees. What was essentially robbery of Jews had become legal when Jews were forced on February 21, 1939, to turn in all jewelry of any value. Fortunately, the courage and loyalty of former employees were able to access and ship some of the jewelry Ida had left behind as part of her former husband's private collection.

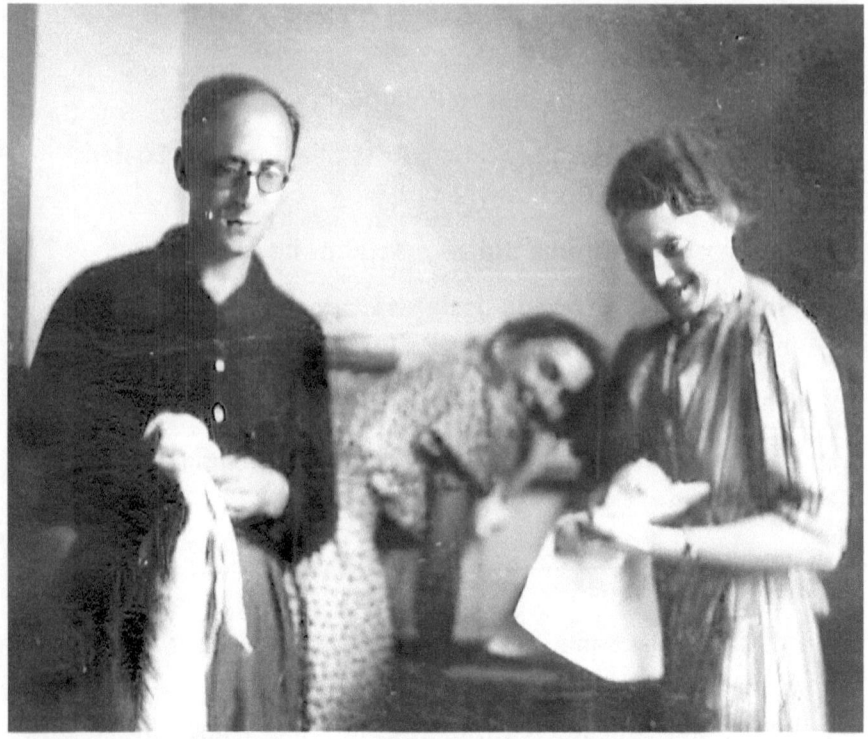
Paul, Margo, and Ida in their London flat, 1939

They went frequently to the cinema to improve their English. They went to friends' homes for tea. They played bridge. Paul hunched over his typewriter. It's difficult to stay calm in the chime of a clock that clicks steadily down. They prepared for life-after-England while feeling thoroughly unmoored. Superficially at least, they lived a life of seeming equanimity. Margo's penchant for equanimity naturally ran deep, while Paul was always in quiet turmoil.

They corresponded with their British friends who had helped them in the past, thanking them. Paul talked of how much he liked England, the spirit and intellect of its people and its traditions of law and orderly government, and expressed his wish to stay. They related with special thanks to A. G. Fallowfield, the British Consul General in Köln, "who clearly saved their lives," as Eric Koch said years later.

Ernst and Lisbeth left behind

Lisbeth, greatly frazzled by the loss of their family home and the departure of first Illa and then Paul and Margo, busied herself packing up crates of belongings and furnishings from Paul and Margo's recently vacated home. She prepared them for shipment to London where they could later be shipped on to the United States once an address was known. She was very methodical (a lawyer's daughter and a doctor's wife-and a thoroughly stern German), but busied herself in the disturbed and distracted way of someone experiencing loss and trauma. She and Paul wrote back and forth about what should be packed, what could be left behind, and "does the umbrella go with the radio."

After the crates were finally sealed, which had to be done in front of a Customs officer, and sent to the harbor in Hamburg, they were told by the shipping firm that Customs wants to open them up again. Lisbeth had a very distraught time of it, much on her own, and as it turns out, to no avail. None of the crates, the umbrella, the radio, and Paul's framed 1931 diploma from the University of Köln ever arrived in London.

***

Ernst and Lisbeth wrote to Paul and Margo several times each week, numbering eighty-nine letters for the entire year. These are full of muted domestic patter, essentially daily updates of their muted life. Each begins *Meine lieben Kinder* ("My dear children") and ends *Und Gute Nacht, liebe Kinder, und einem Jeden von Euch einen herzlichen Küss* ("And a good night, dear children, and to each a heartfelt kiss.")

"*Meine Lieben*," Paul wrote his parents. "My dear ones…" Throughout this year in London, Paul tried to secure the emigration of his parents to a safer place. They explored several possibilities. Perhaps Ernst's service as a military physician in the Great War could be useful in the US, perhaps teaching medical students in the practice of emergency field medicine. Perhaps Ernst could claim he was born a US citizen because his father Adolf had become a US citizen, and perhaps with proper documentation he could thereby secure an impossibly scarce exit visa. Perhaps, perhaps, perhaps.

The Nazi system did what it knew how to do: stall, fabricate, divert, and with every opportunity, say no.[20]

Institutional inertia and corruption even struck allegedly friendly and supportive organizations. There was an endless back and forth with the German Jewish Aid Committee (of the United Kingdom), which always wanted more information and more assurance that Ernst and ELisbeth wouldn't be a burden. Paul enlisted the Dutch Committee for Jewish Refugees for help, which connected Paul to *Eerste Nederlandse* Insurance Co, which finally secured funds, and then for some reason there was a snafu with the Dutch insurance, and Paul sought an interview with the German Jewish Aid Committee, and then… war broke out, then no interview was granted, and all the Committee could do was return the application materials-but not the money.

The letters from Ernst and Lisbeth in 1939 tell of official harassment-blocked bank accounts, and authorities pointing to each other when asked to remove the blocks. Necessary papers didn't arrive, or were late. Their new Köln landlord pushed them out, so they had to

---

20 The bureaucratic Nazi instinct runs deep, still active even sixty years later when I went to the German Embassy in Washington, DC to secure the return of my German citizenship (guaranteed by post-war German law upon presentation of proper evidence), and the European Union passport that comes with it. After presenting all the necessary papers, I was turned away in malfeasant Nazi bureaucratic style. "Come back when you have the name of the ship your parents arrived on," I was told. I left, tail between my legs. It took a while before I realized I'd been played the same way my grandparents had been. Knowing the name of the ship my parents arrived on is in no way required information, confirmed later when the German Consulate in Chicago did its duty, delivered with a genuine apology for their Washington colleagues' behavior. But those fucking Nazis are still around…

move their diminishing household again. At the end of 1939, Hitler demanded that Jews must turn in all their fungible assets. "Legalized theft," there's no other term. Ernst was ill with stomach problems and hospitalized for a short time. Two acquaintances committed suicide.

My parents couldn't bring themselves, in the years after the war, to read these letters again.

War again breaks out in Europe

Finally, Great Britain was virtually forced to declare war against Germany in September 1939 when Prime Minister Chamberlain had to acknowledge that Germany's invasion of Poland meant he'd failed to find "peace in our time," something he'd promised just days earlier. This declaration of a militarized war, not just an administrative, diplomatic, financial, ideological, finger-waving war, lurched Britain into a different mode, and civilian evacuations began from cities to the countryside.

Fortunately, and just in time, just before Germany invaded Poland, Paul and Margo were issued visas to leave Britain and travel to the US. The British and American bureaucratic wheels finally turned in their favor. The US issued them a quota immigration visa in September, and on December 19 the American consulate in London issued a US identification card linking Paul and Margo to the immigration visa. This, finally, was their legal way out.

The time between September 1939 and June 1940 was called a "phony war" by the British media. It may have been phony to those living to the west of Germany. The real action, at least on land, was to the east, in Poland especially, which Germany conquered in short order using its famous tactic of *Blitzkrieg* ("lightning war"). When sufficiently dead, Poland was then divvied up with the Soviet Union, which had also attacked Finland to grab useful territory and important access to international waters to its west.

In western Europe, the war in late 1939 was carried out at sea, in the North Atlantic where the Nazi navy tried to strangle the UK by sinking cargo ships in an effort to isolate the entire British Isles and cut them off from shipments of material and food. On January 8, 1940, the food situation was sufficiently dire that the British government began food rationing.

Paul and Margo, with new visas in hand, secured steamship tickets to leave Britain for the United States on January 24, 1940.

Paul and Margo settle the New World as the Nazis pursue

"We can go now," said Margo. "I've got the typewriter," said Paul.

Paul and Margo had a farewell dinner with Ida, Margo's mother. "*Auf weidersehen*, my dear daughter and son-in-law. I look forward to joining you over there in due course. I don't know how long I'm to stay here. My visa is different from yours, and no one knows how all this will play out. The same is true for Erich Otto, and how long he can remain a student at Cambridge is unknown. Thank goodness Robert is now safe in New Orleans with our relatives there. As for my own mother, rattling around alone in that great house in the West End, who knows…? She lost her husband and one son in the Great War, and has grieved most of her life. But let's not dwell on that. It's time for you to go."

Resisting departure the whole way, Paul fell ill that night with a fever of 106.2F, and in the morning was taken by ambulance with Margo all the way from London to the port at Southampton. They boarded a tender which took them to the big ship, the SS Veendam of the Holland-America line. In his daybook he insisted he wasn't sea-sick, but Margo says he was ill most of the way. Paul always said the ocean has curative powers for him.

Twelve days later, February 5, 1940, the SS Veendam docked at Hoboken, New Jersey, delivering Paul and Margo to their new world. (The famous Ellis Island immigration facility closed years earlier when immigration had been reduced by Congress to a trickle.)

And at the dock they were met by family! Margo's cousins Hans Kahn and Eva Kahn met them at the boat and took them by car to their home in Upper Montclair, New Jersey, where their Papa Emil had been appointed to the music faculty at Montclair State Teachers College. Their younger brother Wolf, in England thanks to a *kindertransport* train, planned to join them later in April.

A few days after arriving and staying with the Montclair Kahns, Paul and Margo reached for their own foothold in America and rented an apartment in Manhattan. It was a cold water walk-up, an apartment at 151 W. 84th St., later described as a hellhole. They lived there more than a year while trying to get their feet on the ground.

Margo found a job as an office stenographer and typist and learned to operate a telephone switchboard. Paul found work as well joining Harry I. Winkler Co., an import-export company downtown.[21] But in June, he wrote that because trans-Atlantic shipping was jeopardized by the Nazi fleet and deemed risky, "business is terrible."

Hot war in all of western Europe and Africa

Newsreel (1940)

January 8—Rationing begins in Britain.

April 9—Nazis invade Denmark and Norway.

May 10—Nazis invade France, Belgium, Luxembourg and the Netherlands.

May 26—Evacuation of Allied troops from Dunkirk begins.

June 14—Germans enter Paris.

July 10—Battle of Britain begins.

---

21   Harry Winkler, also a German Jewish refugee, was soon to become the father of Henry Winkler. If things had played out differently, I could have grown up friends with "The Fonz."

July 23–Soviets take Lithuania, Latvia and Estonia.

August 15–Air battles and daylight raids over Britain.

August 17–Hitler declares a blockade of the British Isles.

August 23/24–First German air raids on Central London.

August 25/26–First British air raid on Berlin.

September 15–Massive German air raids on London, Southampton, Bristol, Cardiff, Liverpool and Manchester.

September 16–United States military conscription bill passed.

November 5–Roosevelt re-elected as U.S. president.

November 14/15–Germany bombs Coventry, England.

November 20–Hungary and then Romania join the Axis Powers.

December 9/10–British begin a western desert offensive in North Africa against the Italians.

December 29/30–Massive German air raid on London.

In April, with Paul and Margo now safely in the US, the 1940 Newsreel's events come to life. The Nazis struck to the west, and the war went from "phony" to extremely real. In April Germany invaded Denmark and Norway. In May they invaded France, Belgium, Luxembourg, and the Netherlands. The German *Wehrmacht* ("defense force") rolled in and took all those countries with little effective resistance. In each, Nazi Germany installed its own occupation government. The US looked on with trepidation and a wish to not get involved.

In full command of France, Hitler grandly toured the prized city of Paris, his troops fully occupying the city's cafes and restaurants, as well as all the nation's formal institutions. Paul and Margo were outraged.

In July, Hitler hurled his air force at the UK, beginning the "battle of Britain," with air battles, massive bombing all through August and September of the populous center of London, and daylight raids over Britain including manufacturing and civilian centers in Southampton, Bristol, Cardiff, Liverpool and Manchester, and in November the cathedral city of Coventry, with a massive raid of London in the last days of 1940.

Ida, in London at age fifty-one, did battle with the fucking Nazis herself on the city's rooftops, serving as an air raid warden during the German *Luftwaffe*'s massive bomb drops. London was hardly a strategic target but was chosen to inflict terror. Ida worked the rooftops and helped calm people in the nearby underground subway station. Knowing her, I can imagine her being good at that, and we still keep her gas mask case.

In New York, Paul readied himself for national service.

In October 1940, he wrote to his brother-in-law Otto Erich Koch, recently deported from Cambridge and installed in a prison camp in Montreal after being "deemed suspect" as a German citizen. Paul wrote that he Margo's other brother Robert in New Orleans were going to register for the draft the following week. "Aliens with first papers (a Social Security card) are equal to American citizens for that purpose. In the classes of '21 through '35 years every ninth is liable to be drafted, so there's a twenty-two percent chance that either Robert or I shall be soldiers," Paul wrote. This was more than a year before the US entered the war.

The United States, even though out of the war in Europe, was gripped by rising tensions. Enough people were opposed to getting into another far-away war that President Roosevelt was limited to supporting Britain through the Lend-Lease Act in an effort to keep Great Britain supplied but was otherwise restrained throughout the year until the events of early December.

Ernst and Lisbeth at the end of their rope

Paul's parents were still stranded in Köln with no way or means to leave, and with diminished means even to stay. Because the US and Germany were still not at war with each other, Paul and Illa were able to stay in touch with them through the mail.

Still alive in their bubbling lobsterpot, they were squeezed of their last assets by the Nazi regime. They were forced to move out their most recent home and to live very entrapped as renters in a still smaller home, with the realities of Germany in a state of raging war with all of Europe. At least those in the western part of Germany were not touched by the fighting. German propaganda sang of invincibility.

That couldn't last, Paul knew, and he again worked feverishly to create escape routes for his parents, just as he had tried from England. One option was that they somehow travel from Germany to Lisbon to Cuba, a route taken by a stream of other late emigrants. Jousting with his typewriter against unwilling bureaucrats and privateers continued to be an exercise in Kafkaesque futility, Paul's legal skills were up against complete and unfettered Nazi intransigence and their wish to bleed the last Jews dry. Cuba's opportunistic haggling exacted as much money as possible, and then it too closed its doors, but not until April 1942.

Newsreel (1941)

January 22—Tobruk in North Africa falls to the British and Australians.

February 14—First units of German 'Afrika Korps' arrive in North Africa.

April 6—Nazis invade Greece and Yugoslavia, which surren-

der later that month.

May 10/11—Heavy German bombing of London; British bomb Hamburg.

June 22—Germany attacks Soviet Union as Operation Barbarossa begins.

July 3—Stalin calls for a scorched earth policy.

August 20—Nazi siege of Leningrad begins.

September 19—Nazis take Kiev, then Odessa, then Kharkov, then Sevastopol.

September 29—Nazis murder 33,771 Jews at Kiev.

December 5—German attack on Moscow is abandoned. Soviet Army launches a major counter-offensive around Moscow.

Ferocious war in eastern Europe

Throughout 1941, the forces of Nazi Germany maintained their ferocity, having successfully taken all of western Europe except the British Isles (and Switzerland, which it left alone so it could still engage with Swiss banks). They struck forcefully to the East, driving deep into Russia at several points, taking Ukraine along the way.

"Ferocity" is a good word to describe the German character when unleashed, as is "brutality" and "cruelty." When Hitler came to full power in 1933, many in the West were cautiously optimistic that this peculiar strongman could actually help his adopted, potentially great nation live up to its potential. But why all that hatred and bellicosity? It's one thing to be proud of one's country and make its economic and technological genius work in favor of its citizens, heck even Paul was in favor of that, but it's quite another to unleash its inner warlike nature and direct it on a program of full domination of the entire continent, burning and pillaging as it goes.

Their ferocity was on full display in 1941, as the narrative below shows, but because it took place in the Slavic lands to the east, it was little noticed in the west. There was and still is a strong cultural divide in mutual awareness, shall we say, between the West and the East. In the early part of the year, the forces of Nazi Germany launched its fury to the south and east, savaging the Balkans and Greece and getting themselves in position to plunge into Russia, By this time, Hitler wanted Russia's vast resources, despite the "non-aggression pact" that Hitler had signed with Stalin earlier.

In June, Germany broke this pact, and with no announcement or declaration of war, invaded with full-scale attacks, taking Minsk immediately. Stalin then announced a scorched earth policy, but Germany was not deterred, taking Leningrad in August, Kiev in September, Odessa, Kharkov, Sevastopol and Rostov in October and November.

As the *Wehrmacht* advanced into Russia, its war against Jews was also fully aflame. In September alone, in just two days, German forces slaughtered approximately 33,771 Jews during a two-day span in Kiev, the capital of Ukraine. A ravine in Kiev named Babi Yar was filled over a period of several months with the bodies not only of Jews but people of all ethnicities. Ukrainians, Russians, Gypsies and people of all nationalities were murdered there. It is an international gravesite.

The Germans, with help from local Ukrainian collaborators, concealed their crimes by filling in the ravine with dirt. The events of September 29-30 were the largest single massacre to date, but were surpassed the following month in Odessa, where 50,000 Jews were massacred. Germany marched on to take Kharkov, Sevastopol, and Rostov, only to be repulsed finally in December. Mass executions continued at Babi Yar until 1943 when the Nazis evacuated, and Soviet forces liberated Kiev.

On September 26, a notice was posted that "All Yids of the city of Kiev and its vicinity must appear on Monday, 29 September, by eight o'clock in the morning at the corner of Mel'nikova and Dokterivskaya streets (near the Viis'kove cemetery). Bring documents, money and valuables, and also warm clothing, linen, etc. Any Yids who do not follow this order and are found elsewhere will be shot. Any civilians who enter the dwellings left by Yids and appropriate the things in them will be shot."

According to testimony after the war: "I watched what happened when the Jews—men, women and children—arrived. The Ukrainians led them past a number of different places where one after the other they had to give up their luggage, then their coats, shoes and over-garments and also underwear. They also had to leave their valuables in a designated place. There was a special pile for each article of clothing. It all happened very quickly and anyone who hesitated was kicked or pushed by the Ukrainians to keep them moving. ...

"Once undressed, they were led into the ravine which was about one hundred and fifty meters long and thirty meters wide and a good fifteen meters deep .. When they reached the bottom of the ravine, they were seized by members of the *Schutzpolizei* and made to lie down on top of Jews who had already been shot .. The corpses were literally in layers. A police marksman came along and shot each Jew in the neck with a submachine gun.. I saw these marksmen stand on layers of corpses and shoot one after the other .. The marksman would walk across the bodies of the executed Jews to the next Jew, who had meanwhile lain down, and shoot him."

Always sensitive to image, Germany immediately concealed these crimes, and they stayed concealed a long time. If the American public knew of this, it's possible it would have felt outraged enough to encourage US entry into the war. Paul and other Americans probably didn't know about them until they were revealed when Soviet forces liberated Kiev at the end of 1943.

The US is bombed and enters the war

Newsreel (late 1941)

December 7–Japan bombs Pearl Harbor, Hawaii, base of the US Pacific fleet.

December 8–United States and Britain declare war on Japan.

December 11–Hitler declares war on the United States.

December 19–Hitler takes complete control of the German Army.

Nazi leadership felt their good fortunes beginning to slip away in late 1941. On December 5, 1941 (no one except Japan knew this was two days before its surprise attack on the US at Pearl Harbor) the Soviet Army forced Germany to abandon its attack on Moscow and launched a major counter-offensive. This was a clear sign that Germany had over-extended itself militarily. Hitler was losing support among his veteran generals who had warned him earlier to tamp down his ambitions.

Deciding to show confidence, Hitler issued the "Night and Fog Decree," in which all those under his command suspected of underground activities, rather than be taken as hostages, would now be made to vanish without a trace into the night and fog, and no information would be given as to their fate or whereabouts. Victims were mostly from France, Belgium, and Holland. This was seen by many as a sign that Hitler himself no longer *felt* in command, and that he was mentally losing his grip.

Suddenly, the course of the war dramatically and unalterably changed. Two fateful decisions were made. The first was not by Hitler but by his ally Emperor Hirohito of Japan. On "a day that will live in infamy," December 7, 1941, Japan without warning attacked the US fleet at anchor in Pearl Harbor, Hawaii. This shook Main Street America to its core, and on December 8, President Franklin D. Roosevelt was finally able to ask Congress to declare war on Japan, which it did (with one vote against). Great Britain jumped in the same day.

In the second decision, Hitler, in another sign of derangement, decided to embrace his like-minded ally Japan, whom he'd never even met, with an enthusiastic gesture of solidarity, and declared war on the US. He seemed to be dismissing the incredible resources that the US would undoubtedly bring to the fight. He also seemed to be ignoring the struggles his own troops were enduring in the east, where they were for the first time being beaten back by a very angry Soviet army also known as fierce, brutal, and cruel. Italy also declared war on the US. On December 11, four days after the attack by Japan, both Germany and Italy declared war on the United States. That finally allowed Congress to return the favor and declare war on them.

The decision by Hitler to declare war on the US, opening a second front while it was being forced into retreat on its first front in Russia, is often seen as Hitler's biggest strategic mistake. Indeed, the tide turned. It's entirely possible that if Hitler hadn't done so, the US would not have entered the war in Europe.

***

Entering the war meant that all mail service to Germany was stopped immediately. A letter to his parents in Köln postmarked in New York on December 6 came back, "Return to sender." A letter from Köln to Paul and Margo in New York on December 10 was recovered and is the last letter from Ernst and Lisbeth in Paul's Archives. Isolation was complete. More of the "silent scream."

Not only was communication cut off, but so was all possibility of escape from Germany, at least by legal means (which was the only means these Mayers allowed themselves to contemplate.)

Beginning in late 1941, Jews were actually forbidden to leave Germany. Until then, the campaign to rid Germany of its Jews had been largely one of "encouraging" them to leave, without, as we've seen, their property, rights, and dignity. In the three years since Paul left his parents behind in Germany, he never flagged in his efforts to rescue them. Now the doors were completely shut. There was no means of communication, and their fate was almost entirely invisible and unknowable for the duration of the war.

Paul had no hesitation in standing up for his new country. He was eager to help prosecute this war, which he knew was bound to be catastrophic, and take it to his enemy.

He could have avoided military service, a man his age with a disqualifying punctured eardrum if he acknowledged it (disqualifying for the infantry). And while the import-export business was terrible at the time, he knew it would prosper if and when the war came to a successful conclusion.

There was a tradition of service in Paul's family. His father had served his country and Kaiser as a field doctor in the Great War of 1914-1918. His grandfather Adolf had served the US as a new arrival just before its Civil War, enlisting in the Union infantry, and becoming a citizen of the US. And his great-grandfather Samuel had served his people and his King in Hechingen as a rabbi, civil rights lawyer, and aide to the Hohenzollern Prince.

Paul had already registered for the draft, as had all the males in his and Margo's extended US-based family. He was now thirty-five, with a wife, a meager base of support, not yet a citizen and with the dubious status of an "immigrant refugee." He would be leaving his thirty year-old wife, who fortunately had a job and impeccable social skills with a supportive boss and a community of immigrant refugee friends.

But he wanted to be part of this fight. He knew this was his war. He went downtown to the recruiting office, took an oath.

The US goes all-in, and Paul reports for duty (1942)

Newsreel (early 1942)

January 13—Germany begins a U-boat offensive along east coast of USA.

January 20—SS Leader Heydrich holds the Wannsee Conference to coordinate the "Final Solution of the Jewish Question."

January 26—First American forces arrive in Great Britain.

April 23—German air raids begin against cathedral cities in Britain.

May 26—Rommel begins an offensive in North Africa against the Gazala Line.

May 30—First thousand-bomber British air raid (against Köln).

June—Mass murder of Jews by gassing begins at Auschwitz.

June 5—Germans besiege Sevastopol.

June 10—Nazis liquidate Lidice in reprisal for Heydrich's assassination.

June 21—Rommel captures Tobruk.

Having been forced to declare war on both sides of the Atlantic, the US immediately ramped up mobilization dramatically. It had to rebuild its fleet in the Pacific to fight against Imperial Japan's impending assault of its West Coast. And it had to build up its Atlantic fleet to keep Germany away from its East Coast, aid the defense of Great Britain, and prepare invasions of Africa and continental Europe to dislodge the forces of Nazi Germany. It had to create enough air power to support both those missions. And, of course, it had to recruit the power of American men and women and train them for military as well as civilian duties to supply goods and material to both fronts. It was a massive effort, well-supported and well-organized, and hugely successful. Thank you, America.

Germany now had its hands full on its eastern and western fronts, and engaged with new urgency. After joining the war against the US, Hitler thought it important to put himself in charge of his entire military.

Amidst all the hell of warfare, Germany picked up its pace to "rid Europe of Jews from east to west." Reinhard Heydrich, second in command of the SS (*Schutzstaffel*), the elite paramilitary guard of the Nazi regime and a virtual state within the Third Reich, was put in charge. He convened a conference in the Berlin suburb of Wannsee in the beginning of 1942. At the meeting, fifteen top Nazi bureaucrats and members of the SS met to coordinate the "Final Solution" in which the Nazis would attempt to exterminate the eleven million Jews of Europe and the Soviet Union.

Ernst and ELisbeth deported to Czechoslovakia

"We just heard from them! Papa and Mama say they're healthy and happy." Despite the shutdown of official mail service across the Atlantic, one post card got through via the German Red Cross. On June 5, Dr Ernst "Israel" Mayer und Frau wrote an almost cheerful Springtime letter to Paul on official Red Cross form stationery where they were limited to twenty-five words. "We are healthy and happy. Enjoy the beautiful nature. Hope you're well satisfied. Somewhat belated cordial *Pfingsten* kiss." *Pfingsten*, Whitsun or Pentecost in English, is observed throughout Europe as a Christian or at least Springtime holiday.

Two weeks after celebrating the descent of the Holy Spirit upon the disciples of Jesus celebrated at *Pfingsten*, the grotesque *Gestapo* (the State Secret police) began their work on the Wannsee agenda and knocked hard on Dr. Ernst "Israel" Mayer's door. This time there was no way to deter or refuse them, and no escape.

On June 16, Ernst (age sixty-seven) and ELisbeth (age fifty-eight) were taken from their home by the SS, who were charged with co-ordinating the deportation of Jews to ghettos, concentration camps and killing sites.

Some, such as Ernst and Lisbeth, were taken and "concentrated" with others on the outskirts of Köln for several days before those in charge could marshal enough rail cars together to ship them efficiently further east. Most of those rounded up were sent to extermination camps (aka death camps or killing sites). Germany used six such camps, all in Poland-Auschwitz-Birkenau, Sobibor, Treblinka, Majdanek, Chelmno, and Belzec.

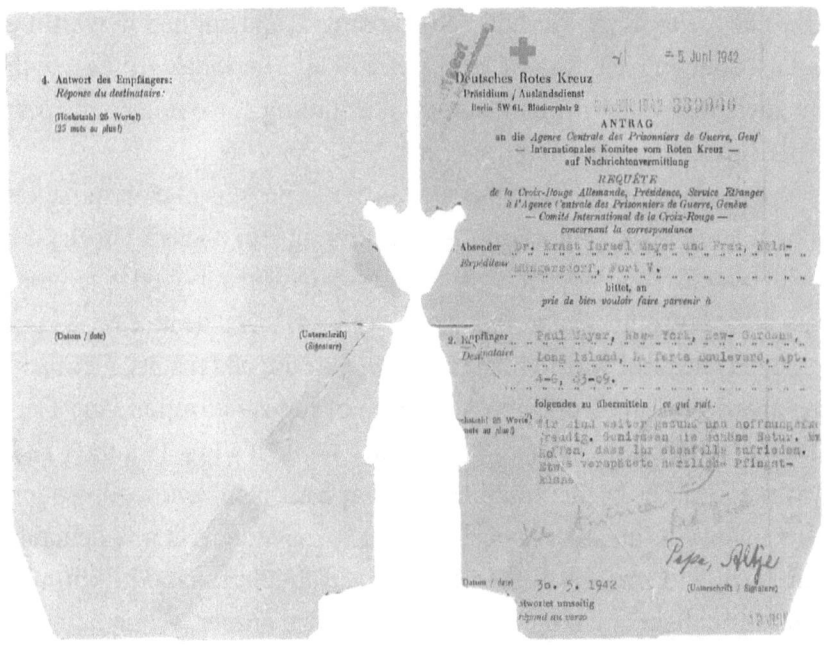

Message from Ernst and Lisbeth, June 5, 1942, via German Red Cross.

The distinction between concentration camps and death camps is crucial, though often glossed over. Says Wikipedia, "The National Socialists made no secret of the existence of concentration camps as early as 1933, as they served as a deterrent to resistance. The extermination camps, on the other hand, were kept strictly secret. To disguise the mass murder, even in internal correspondence, they only referred to it as "special treatment," "cleansing," "resettlement," or "evacuation." The SS referred to the extermination camps as concentration camps. Their internal organizational structures were also largely identical. The term "extermination camp" was only used later in historical scholarship and in court cases and serves to further categorize the camps.... The idea of mass extermination with the use of stationary facilities, to which the victims were taken by train, was the result of earlier Nazi experimentation with chemically manufactured poison gas during the secretive Aktion T4 euthanasia programme against hospital patients with mental and physical disabilities. The technology was adapted, expanded, and applied in wartime to unsuspecting victims of many ethnic and national groups, with the Jews being the primary target, accounting for over ninety percent of extermination camp victims."[22]

I'm not going to relate the horrors of this process of extermination known later as the Holocaust ("burnt offering," in ancient Greek). Its scale, brutality, and impact even on those few who survived is remembered like few other events in history. "Industrialized death camps" is a sanitized and brief way to relate its style, purpose and results. Germany has always led the world in its mastery of industrialization, and Germans were certainly masters of this one. While it's true that their task was made easier by the often eager or at least compliant cooperation of non-Jews in all the Slavic lands east of Germany, it's undeniable that Nazified Germany was in charge, and they managed to kill millions through orders of the SS before the Allied armies, acting lawfully through their governments, stopped them. After the war, the new government of Germany apologized. It was the least they could do.

Anyone interested in this gruesome but still recent subject can find it on the internet by searching "Nazis and the Holocaust," or

---

22 Wikipedia, "Extermination camp"

"How allegedly decent people came to follow the Nazis," or "What made the Nazis so horrible?" The fewest results, I'll bet, can be found by searching, "What can be done to prevent the next Holocaust?"

***

Travelling to one of these "camps" (I still have a hard time calling it a "camp") was not the *immediate* fate of Ernst and Lisbeth. Their fate was slow to unfold after they were snatched from their home in Köln for deportation. After ten days in a holding pen by the railyard on the edge of town, they were shipped to Theresienstadt, a fortress town in the Sudetenland in the northern province of Czechoslovakia, annexed by the Nazis in 1938. Official records kept by the Nazis show Ernst was shipped from Köln with transport III/1 on 16.6.1942, his train number was 919. ELisbeth was deported the same day but a different train, number 920.

One has to wonder what Ernst and Lisbeth were doing the day the Gestapo knocked on their door. Did they know their arrest was coming—*really* know? The Gestapo had come for them several years earlier, but Ernst had sent them away, saying "I can't go with you. I have patients to treat." This time, however, the Gestapo felt free to carry out its orders.

Theresienstadt (Terezin in Czech) was an unusual destination for rail cars headed East from Germany. It was designed as a transfer post, not an extermination camp but a "camp-ghetto," or "show camp" for Jews too prominent to kill immediately. As a show camp, resident Jews were made to perform for German filmmakers eager to show how well the Nazis treated them[23] Between June 2 and the end of the war in April 1945, 58,087 Jews were sent there, first from Germany, Austria, and Czechoslovakia, later from Netherlands, Poland and Denmark. Throughout this time, the Nazis were sending trainloads of not so prominent Jews from Theresienstadt to death camps further east.

---

23 More on this later, in *"Mein Kampf, Part II"*

Neither Paul nor Illa learned of their parents' deportation to Theresienstadt until much later. The last they'd heard was that stilted letter from Köln on May 30, 1942. Unknown to them, beginning in October of 1942, four months after their parents' arrival in Theresienstadt, twenty-seven trainloads in twenty-four months (carrying 46,720 Jews) were shipped to Auschwitz-Birkenau alone. Were Ernst and Lisbeth among them? Paul, Illa, and Margo didn't know one way or the other until September 1946, four and half years after they last heard from them, after the war ended.

Paul embraces Army life

Newsreel (middle 1942)

June 25–General Dwight D. Eisenhower arrives in London.

July 5–Soviet resistance in the Crimea ends.

July 9–Germans begin a drive toward Stalingrad in the USSR.

August 7–British General Bernard Montgomery takes command of Eighth Army in North Africa.

August 12–Stalin and Churchill meet in Moscow.

"Keep your head up. I've already met some nice boys," Paul wrote Margo on August 28 on a USO postcard from New York's Penn Station. He was on his way to Ft. Dix, NJ. "This is the first message from the Army..." Dated and marked #1, to Margo at their apartment in Kew Gardens, Long Island.[24] Two weeks earlier, Paul had been inducted into the Army at Ft. Jay, NY, and ordered to report for

---

24 By May of 1941, he and Margo had saved enough to move out of their dingy upper West Side walkup where they shared a bathroom with strangers, and moved into a small apartment in Kew Gardens, in Queens, Long Island (Apartment 4-G, 83-09 Lefferts Blvd).

duty two weeks later. He was on a mission to serve his new country, rescue his parents, release Germany from the grip of the Nazi death cult, and restore his rightful life.

Paul became part of the war effort, and he was glad to go. Earlier in the year, just after the US declared war on Japan across the Pacific and Germany across the Atlantic, the US scrambled to mount a force that could prevail in both Europe and the Pacific against hugely powerful and by now experienced forces that dominated the air, seas, and huge amounts of land. But scramble it did, in probably the most major mobilization efforts ever seen.

Pvt. Paul Mayer, US Army, 1942, age 35

Joining the US Army in a time of war created a whole new life for Paul. He was not so young anymore. At age thirty-five he was always among the oldest in his Army unit, yet he was eager to sign up for the rigors of Army life and fight the Nazis the best way he could. Those years playing soccer in school and tennis well into adulthood had kept him in pretty good shape.

As revealed in his first postcard, in even his first sentence ("Keep your head up, I've already met some nice boys."), Paul showed his eager embrace of Army life and Army language.

He wrote Margo often, two-three letters a week throughout his entire service and asked her to keep them all as an on-going journal of his Army experience. He wrote of his daily experience and his reaction to Army life.

While still at Ft. Dix, not far from NYC, in letter #2, "In the morning I had to work on the garbage. In the afternoon I cleaned all the cigarette butts which the Sunday visitors had left. Later, I hoed weeds and after that we had a retreat which is a kind of parade, everybody in tan uniform. The boys who have been here only three to four days did very well, and it really gives you the impression as if we can beat the Germans. Marching for the first time, behind a flag and accompanied by a band, is really terribly impressive for a man, and I suppose a female would not understand it even if one tried hard to explain."

He liked the food, he said, and he thought KP (Kitchen Patrol) wasn't as bad as others said. "The sergeants and corporals are very good; they are tough, all right, but you always feel they are human; they are good soldiers and one gains the impression as if the army is really in good hands."

And a few days later, "It really was good you were here yesterday. It's something to hold to; after all, the new life here is, say, strange for a married man of my age."

While Paul quickly took to Army life, the Army took a long time to figure out what to do with him, an older inductee given the official designation "enemy alien"—"enemy" because he was from

Germany and "alien" because he was not legally a citizen of the US or any other country.

He became impatient. He wanted to get ahead in rank and to be more useful in the war effort.

On September 10 they sent him to Camp Blanding, near Jacksonville, FL. He invited Margo to come to Florida for a visit. "There is a beautiful lake where we can swim. The food is really good, and although the service seems to become tough, all officers and noncoms take good care and work hard as we do....In our bunk there are all kinds of men, lawyers, salesmen, artists, laborers; stupid ones and intelligent ones, and nobody knows what made the Army send us here."

Camp Blanding was a training site for the Army's Military Police. In typical Army fashion, those in charge thought that Paul, with his training in Law and a doctoral dissertation on the subject of penal reform, could be useful in the Army's Military Police. "This seems bizarre," Margo wrote to friends in New York, "Paul is a lawyer, not a cop." Even though Paul favored good law enforcement in principle, assuming fair laws and fair enforcement as a Weimar lawyer would rightfully assume. But, "Handling drunk and disorderly American servicemen on weekend liberty doesn't play to his strengths," Margo wrote.

While at Blanding, Paul earned a marksman's ribbon, showing the shooting skills he learned hunting birds in Zweifallshammer. He then asked to serve in the infantry, saying he'd be able to "keep up with the boys" in all the physical aspects of basic training even at his age. But his superiors apparently thought otherwise.

Paul wanted to be an officer, and made those wishes known. One would think someone with his education would be chosen for Officer Candidate School, but most likely his status as an "enemy alien" in the US less than three years was a barrier. He later joked that the Army had to assign another recruit just to follow him around and make sure he wasn't doing the enemy's work.

In his Army letters to Margo, he never talked about his parents, only more mundane matters of day-to-day life. It's as if he'd chosen to put them out of his mind in suspended animation until he was a position to act directly and decisively in their fate. The churn of unspoken things carried on in his stomach in the form of frequent *bauchweg* ("intense diarrhea").

In the meantime, his focus was on prosecuting the war. As he said in September 1942, "This letter written on [Jewish] New Year, I could have taken liberty to go to Jax, forty miles away, to go to temple but I think this guard detail is a better service towards the community and myself."

Letters show he made himself useful to others in the barracks-teaching German, unofficially managing the immigration papers of forty-some barracks mates, and the income tax returns (he'd learned the Tax Code) of three officers. He began to complain to Margo about the slow pace and inefficiencies of things. He praised the high quality of the equipment, and he appreciated "American nice," though abhorred its ignorance.

And this endearing note, dated September 30, "*Mein Liebchen*, It's always such a good feeling that I love you and that you are there and always with me. It's a shelter and at the same time a source of very deep joy."

Newsreel–late 1942

More wartime news from the European Theater of Operations, as it was called,[25] late 1942:

August 17–First all-American air attack in Europe.

August 23–Massive German air raid on Stalingrad.

September 2–Rommel driven back by Montgomery in North Africa

---

25 Please, the reader should take little offense that events in the Pacific Theater of Operations get short shrift in this account.

September 13–Battle of Stalingrad begins.

October 18–Hitler orders the execution of all captured British commandos.

November 1–Operation Supercharge to break Axis lines at El Alamein, followed by US invasion of North Africa.

November 11–Germans and Italians invade unoccupied Vichy France.

November 19–Soviet counter-offensive at Stalingrad begins.

December 2–Professor Enrico Fermi sets up an atomic reactor in Chicago.

December 17–British Foreign Secretary Eden tells the British House of Commons of mass executions of Jews by Nazis; U.S. declares those crimes will be avenged.

December 31–Battle of the Barents Sea between German and British ships.

By 1943 the tide of the war was noticeably turning in favor of the Allies. This was enabled by a key feature of this war, the cooperation and collaboration of Allied leadership at the highest levels, notably the United States, Great Britain, Soviet Union, and Canada, travelling long distance and with risk, to meet each other face to face. Churchill and Roosevelt had been in frequent communication since the beginning of the war, first on defending the island nation, and then when the US entered the war and General Eisenhower arrived in Europe (June 1942) to advance plans for the liberation of Europe through an invasion of ground forces, and even post-war planning. Churchill flew to Moscow to meet with Stalin in August 1942. In January 1943, Churchill and Roosevelt met in Casablanca, where Roosevelt announced the war can end only with "unconditional German surrender." In November 1943, Roosevelt, Churchill, and Stalin meet at Teheran where they coordinated their military strategy against the Axis powers and discussed post-war plans.

Post-war occupation planning had already begun. In fact, it began much earlier, even before the US entered the war, as attested in the Atlantic Charter, signed by Great Britain and the United States in August 1941. While this Charter was not a binding treaty it was significant for several reasons. First, it publicly affirmed the sense of solidarity between the US and Great Britain against Axis aggression. Second, it laid out President Roosevelt's Wilsonian vision for the postwar world, one that would be characterized by freer exchanges of trade, self-determination, disarmament, and collective security. Finally, the Charter ultimately served as an inspiration for colonial subjects throughout the Third World, from Algeria to Vietnam, as they fought for independence. Great Britain and the US clearly wanted to avoid the disastrous mistakes they made not many years earlier when they forced Germany to accept onerous terms, first in the Armistice of 1918 and then in the Treaty of 1919. It's quite amazing how this war was prosecuted with such entirely different vision and cooperation than was the First World War.

***

But at this point, Paul definitely felt stuck. Still holding the rank of Private, he wanted to be doing something useful, something to help move this war along, something fitting his skills and motivation. He was stationed at Camp Blanding from September 1942 until April 1943, and became a US Citizen on February 5 (through special legislation passed by Congress to enable a faster path to citizenship for those serving in the military). While an MP, he still served informally as what's known as a "barracks lawyer," helping his mates and superiors with their personal legal issues.

He worked long and hard hours in the barracks and it's clear in the letters he wrote to Margo that he was frustrated he couldn't advance in the Army's ranks. It's not that he wanted rank for rank's sake-well, actually he did care about the status that rank conferred-but even more he wanted to have more influence in the way the war was conducted. But the door to Officer Candidate School never opened for him. He couldn't really understand this, but he once conveyed to Margo the judgment of one of the door-holders, that Paul "wasn't showing sufficient [American-like] leadership skills." Perhaps they preferred that he be working behind a typewriter rather than a gun-and as noted, he was useful in the barracks.

In April 1943, Paul was bumped up to Corporal and sent to Fort Custer (near Battle Creek, MI), to participate in its Occupational Military Police Program. "Occupational Military Police" refers to the kind of law enforcement applied *after military victory leads to the occupation of taken territory*, the larger vision of Military Police.

While always at work of some kind, Paul occasionally took a weekend furlough, some nearby to luxuriate in a hotel bath and bed. How he managed to maneuver this isn't clear. Perhaps it was in return for barracks favors. He was also occasionally able to *rendezvous* with Margo in New York or somewhere accessible-once to conceive their first son when Paul was permitted to celebrate the Fourth of July with a highly recreational weekend in New York.

"I am somewhat overdue," Margo wrote to inform him a few weeks later. This time there was no question of whether to keep this child. Paul and Margo were beginning to feel, as was the general public, that the tide of war was turning, significantly but not yet irreversibly, in the direction of Allied victory, though anything could still happen. They were happy to be starting a family.

Newsreel (early 1943)

January 10—Soviets begin an offensive against the Germans in Stalingrad.

February 2—Germans surrender at Stalingrad in the first big defeat of Hitler's armies, more than a year after its withdrawal from Moscow.

March 2—Germans begin a withdrawal from Tunisia, Africa.

March 16-20—Fierce battle in the Atlantic, with twenty-one Allied merchant ships sunk by German U-boats, revealing the vulnerability of escorted convoys.

April 19—Waffen-SS attacks Jewish resistance in the Warsaw ghetto.

May 7—Allies take Tunisia.

May 13—German and Italian troops surrender in North Africa.

May 16—Jewish resistance in the Warsaw Ghetto ends.

May 16/17—British air raid on the Ruhr.

May 22—Dönitz suspends U-boat operations in the North Atlantic.

June 11—Himmler orders the liquidation of all Jewish ghettos in Poland.

The Army finally recognizes Paul's gifts

As the war progressed with increasing success by the Allies, the Army began to reimagine Paul as an asset. He was now more fully Paul the German who nevertheless brought important skills to the war effort: he spoke German as only a German can, had studied German law at prestigious German universities, understood the depths of German culture and civilization, and had clear opinions about how to deal with the Nazis, maybe even in ways that could eventually, after Allied victory, put Germany back onto better footing with a more sensible legal infrastructure.

In their interactions with him, his superiors evidently saw that Paul could help the Allies avoid the disastrous mistakes they made not many years earlier when they forced Germany to accept onerous terms, first in the Armistice of 1918 and then in the Treaty of 1919.

Newsreel (late 1943)

July 9-22—Allies land in Sicily, then bomb Rome, then capture Palermo, Sicily.

July 25/26—Mussolini arrested and the Italian Fascist government falls.

July 27/28—Allied air raid causes a firestorm in Hamburg.

August 12-17—Germans evacuate Sicily.

September 8—Italian surrender to Allies is announced, followed by Allied landings at Salerno and Taranto.

September 11/12—Germans occupy Rome, and rescue Mussolini.

October 1—Allies enter Naples, Italy.

October 13—Italy declares war on Germany.

November 6—Russians recapture Kiev in the Ukraine.

November 18—Large British air raid on Berlin.

November 28—Roosevelt, Churchill, Stalin meet at Teheran.

December 24-26—Soviets launch offensives on the Ukrainian front.

Just after the miracle of July 4th, the Army began to see a constructive pathway for Paul, one that would lead to service in Military Intelligence. They advanced him to Staff Sergeant and sent him in mid-July for a month's training at The Citadel, a military academy in Charleston, South Carolina known informally then as "the West Point for the Intelligence Services." This sounded promising.

Then in August, they sent him to a unit of the Army Specialized Training Programs at the University of Illinois. There, Paul was tasked to prepare a dissertation that could be useful to a future Allied

Military Government of Occupied Territory. This dissertation was to serve as a blueprint for a piece of post-war civil/legal infrastructure, namely the control of vice. While "vice" was not exactly Paul's area of expertise, it is well known that with knowledge of the vice industry there are many creative avenues one can take or avoid in the creation of a more civilized society.

But take time to write a dissertation? *No, let's invade now* was Paul's adamant thought, first-born on the way or not. As important as vice control might actually be down the road, writing a dissertation did nothing to get Paul more quickly in position to save his parents or bring the Nazis to their knees. While "Military Intelligence" sounded promising, Paul was chomping at the bit to do something more useful than write a dissertation, no matter how connected "vice control" might be to events once the war was won.

Paul took a few courses in political science and was advised in his dissertation by Dr. J.M. Mathews, an emerging star in the field of international reconstruction. He finished his work in just a few months, and was awarded his second doctorate, a Ph.D. in political science at the University of Illinois, Champaign-Urbana. This dissertation was a meticulous presentation of Paul's legalistic mind and training, and how new, de-Nazified law enforcement protocols could work in the hands of an Office of Civil Affairs of a victorious Military Government. One has to wonder how much the memory of his great-grandfather, the Dr. Rabbi Samuel Mayer, influenced him in his approach to this dissertation.

A breakthrough!

Finally came the opportunity which I like to think was cued up for Paul even before he was sent to The Citadel and University of Illinois. Still a staff sergeant, he was selected by US Army Intelligence Corp and ordered to report on December 3, 1943, to Military Intelligence Training Center, Camp Ritchie, for assignment. Placed in charge of thirteen others for the trip there, he gave Margo his new address as Company E, 2nd Training Battalion, Camp Ritchie, Maryland.

"But I can't say anything about what's going on." That sounded even more promising!

We have to wonder how much Paul knew about Camp Ritchie before reporting there, but by the time the war was over Company E had become famous as "The Ritchie Boys." This was a unit recently formed with German-speaking immigrants to the US who had a shared interest in destroying Nazism. Paul's group was trained to interrogate captured German officers, primarily to gain intelligence on the likely military plans of a German Army now in serious retreat, as well as the condition of the German civil and command structure they were just forced to abandon. In due course, this most interesting unit of military service played a pivotal role in winning the war, as has been documented in books, movies, and TV shows. [26]

Its setting was like something in a movie, too, in the Catoctin Mountains, eighteen miles from Hagerstown, Maryland, and seventy miles from Washington, DC, ideal for the type of secret training that would take place, yet still easy to reach from the Pentagon.

Opened quite early in the US Army's participation in the war, June 19, 1942, it was the first facility for centralized intelligence training in the history of the US, graduating its first class of thirty-three German speaking "students" in October. The commanding officer of the Camp had the authority to transfer to Camp Ritchie any personnel from any branch of the Army possessing knowledge of a foreign language. Pentagon keypunch operators sorted through tens of thousands of punch cards to find soldiers whose records indicated foreign language fluency. That's how they found Paul, but it's not clear when. The data were in his records from the beginning, perhaps they were cultivating him, giving him experience as an

---

26 See 'Ritchie Boys' Aided Army's Efforts to Defeat Germany During WWII, https://www.defense.gov/News/Feature-Stories/story/Article/2064692/ritchie-boys-aided-armys-efforts-to-defeat-germany-during-wwii/

MP, then moving through an Intelligence/Law sequence. Anyway, Ritchie was ready for him when he arrived.

***

We pause at this point for important news on the home front. In July 1943, Margo's mother, still in England, was granted a US visa allowing her to join her daughter and her brother Emil's family already in the New York area. In September, she sailed from England in the midst of a raging maritime war in the North Atlantic, traveling in a darkened convoy protected by US Navy destroyers. Even with protection, these convoys were still very much at risk of attack.

Ida safely arrived in New York on October 10th and was met by her daughter who announced she was pregnant. It is hard to imagine their joy at finally being able to start their new lives in America with a new baby. A few days later, Ida sat down and wrote to Paul, Robert and Eric an excited tale of adventurous travel. It's such a marvelous letter (in her first use of English in America) it must be included here in its entirety, with an addendum by Margo, dated October 14, 1943, Kew Gardens, L.I., N.Y.

> Darling Paul, Robert and Eric,
>
> I can't tell you what a sensation it was to talk to you over the phone. And how thrilled I am to be here, and how marvelous I find everything. I have not been as happy for a long time. And as for becoming a grandmother–I am looking forward to that immensely! I thought it might come nine months or more after my arrival, but as for being as quick as all that … I guessed something like it from Margo's looks at the pier, then she told me immediately we got home… Well, so I am even more glad to be here. The flat is awfully nice, but I shall be glad when we get something bigger… my luggage

came last night, now imagine me with the twelve pieces around me, rather in despair where to put the most vital things. But that problem too will be solved.

I shall use Eric's letter as a kind of *Fragebogen* ("questionnaire"), as it was so full of questions. No, my nerves are not shattered at all; the three weeks' trip with nothing to do was restful enough, in spite of the strain. One gets used to everything, and I slept very well even! No, our convoy was not attacked, but we knew about the attack on the other one of course, by radio, and that made us make a big detour and accounts for the delay partly. We had boat-drills etc. every few days, where it was decided who had to go with whom in the boats, which were always being equipped with food. We had to have our equipment always handy. One gets fatalistic; I cant say I was afraid; the Blitz in London may account for that. I undressed at night, and I think most people did. All doors had to be kept wide open day and night, they were fixed *sperrangelweit* ("wide open"), so that they could not jam and trap you in a case of emergency. I had about four days in London to get ready; on the 15th, when I sent you the photos, Eric, I knew it, but was not absolutely sure. Two days later I left Uncle L. who was most awfully down and unhappy–I cant bear thinking of it–Olga and Mr. Kahn saw me off, and the Poppers who live near Cardiff spent the last evening with me for dinner at my hotel, so I was not alone. After embarking and sailing for a few hours it took a few days until the convoy was assembled. It was a big one, and that is a marvellous sight. I succeeded in getting a cabin to myself which was lucky. I did not know anybody on board, but happened, without my "*Zutun*"("doing anything") of course, to be placed at the best table, the Captain's table, together with two American journalists and the Mexican Ambassador in London with his wife. That was a very nice and interesting set, we had lots of good conversations, played bridge regularly etc. Most of the other people (seventy passengers altogether) were refugees, mostly from Austria and Tschecoslovakia. One soon got to know each other. For a few days it was very cold, we all thought we were near the North Pole. The last days again were very warm, and the approach to the Skyline and the arrival were absolutely glorious. We were not taken to Ellis Island but had to stay on board until all formalities were done with, the following afternoon (Sunday). I managed to get word to Margo later Saturday night, she came to the pier about noon on Sunday, where she could see me, but not talk to me until we were released, about four hours later. That had been the first night without blackout, that <u>was</u> lovely! No, there had been no restrictions about being on deck, there were planes overhead on the British coast and then the last days here, not between. Food was not too good on board, but plentiful. It was a South African boat, rather a small one, the whole crew were coloured men, East-Indians. I hope to tell you more details soon when I see you. I wonder if Robertlein can really manage soon? It would be lovely. I am still skeptic about Canada, but shall of course try everything; so far nobody could give me any precise information. I have already applied for my first papers, and have seen and spoken to a number of people, Martha Heiden etc., the Jacobis over the phone, Emil and Mathilda came here, Wolf last night too-it is really marvellous how he has changed–I can't say much about Mathilda yet, but so far she seems alright, now I must hurry to meet Fritz Fl with whom I am going to see his mother in Flushing, that's why I must stop, and will give you my New York impressions next time. I get along alright. The food of course is marvellous, and a pleasure every day, I have never enjoyed it as much. All the best, I hear you never got my birthday letter Paul, what a pity.

Yours, Mutti.

Then Margo appended:

This is me, Margo. I just came home and found Mother's letter to you all, and would like to add a few things. The most important thing: She has not changed in the least which was an enormous relief. I had always been somewhat afraid that the Blitz and everything else might have spoilt something, but it has not. She looks splendid, and everybody compliments me on her. You cant imagine how happy we are together, it is a terrific change in my life and no end of relief. I have no doubt that she will very soon be quite used to this new life, she has not lost her old vitality and energy, and I can leave her alone quite safely, she always gets where she wants! Those last weeks of worry and anxiety are over and forgotten, but I keep getting phone calls from all kinds of people, telling me that they had not dared calling me up before, from fear of getting bad news.–I hope to get a larger apartment in this house around Dec 1. We are somewhat crammed at present, but we can manage somehow.–No need to tell you that her grandson [in utero] is also pleased to know her around, it is a great pleasure and relief for him, and they get on very well together. So far he is not too conspicuous, but that will soon change. He is behaving most reasonably at present, much better than sometime ago.

M.

What spirit!
Happy days ahead!

Later that same week, a letter was received from the International Red Cross in London and New York to the American Red Cross, Greenville, Mississippi, responding to an inquiry sent ten months earlier, notifying Illa that the addresses of their parents is Theresienstadt, in the German Protectorate of Bohemia and Moravia in Czechoslovakia.

So much for seamless transitions to wondrous days. War time was still war time.

***

A few weeks later, Paul reported to Ritchie.

By the time Paul arrived on the evening of December 10, 1943, a camp theater had been constructed for propaganda training sessions, which would one day include mock Nazi rallies with a Hitler look-alike. For instruction in conducting raids and house searches while avoiding enemy booby traps, an authentic-looking German village was built, its facades resembled the back lot of a Hollywood film studio. This was all done even before the first students arrived, with a level of security second only to that given to the development of the atomic bomb at the Manhattan Project, which started that same summer in Oak Ridge, Tennessee.

The first eight-week class at Camp Ritchie graduated thirty-three German-speaking students in October 1942 from a course called Interrogation of Prisoners of War (IPW). Thereafter, the classes became much larger, and a new one started each month. The thirty-four classes that followed graduated on average five hundred students per month.[27] Most of Camp Ritchie's German-speaking European immigrants specialized in interrogation training.

The principles of interrogation taught at Ritchie were very advanced. They were trained in non-violent interrogation methods that

---

27 Bruce Henderson, *Sons and Soldiers: The Untold Story of the Jews Who Escaped the Nazis and Returned with the U.S. Army to Fight Hitler*, Harper Audio, 2017.

were then and are still considered the gold standard of interrogation techniques.[28] Their instruction was based on lectures by Sanford Griffiths, an interrogator (for the British) in WWI. After the war he had studied psychology, persuasion, and marketing. These principles melded well with principles of successful interrogation.[29]

Griffiths outlined sixteen principles for a successful "interview."[30]

1. Try to see things from the prisoner's point of view.
2. Avoid preconceived attitudes, like "All Germans are Nazis, they can't be trusted."
3. Germans are people, not superheroes
4. Take an individual approach. "What is he suffering, what does he want?"
5. Get at them when they're shaky. They have a will to live.
6. Intimate subjects like religion may reveal some common feelings.
7. Hide your focus of attention, don't suggest the answers you're looking for.
8. Use potential relations, one solder at the front to another, pal to pal, one musician to another.
9. Make a good first impression.
10. Make close name and interest identification
11. Bait the hook to suit the fish.

---

28   Beverley Driver Eddy, *Ritchie Boy Secrets: How a Force of Immigrants and Refugees Helped Win World War II*. Rowland and Littlefield, 2021.
29   See Henderson, *op cit.* and Eddy, *op cit.*
30   One should note how significantly different these principles are from those adopted by the US in the 21st century for use in its so-called war on terror– such as "waterboarding."

12. Let the prisoner tell us.
13. Don't look for repentant Nazis. Do not put on air of moral superiority.
14. Listen to prisoner's complaints.
15. Use some propaganda as a softener.
16. Give them paradoxes to worry about. "If Germans are invincible, why are you losing?"

Newsreel (early 1944)

January 6–Soviet troops advance into Poland.

January 22–Allies land at Anzio in Italy.

January 27–Leningrad relieved after a 900-day siege.

February 15-18–Allies bomb the monastery at Monte Cassino, Italy; Germans counterattack against the Anzio beachhead.

March 4–Soviet troops begin an offensive on the Belorussian front; first major daylight bombing raid on Berlin by the Allies.

March 18–British drop 3000 tons of bombs during an air raid on Hamburg, Germany.

April 8–Soviet troops begin an offensive to liberate Crimea; Germany surrenders May 12.

May 25–Germans retreat from Anzio.

June 5–Allies enter Rome.

June 6–D-Day landings on the northern coast of France.

June 10–Nazis liquidate the town of Oradour-sur-Glane in France.

June 13–First German V-1 rocket attack on Britain.

June 27–US troops liberate Cherbourg, France.

1944, the Allies storm continental Europe

By early 1944, the Allies had turned the tide, especially in the East after the Russian winter took its toll on the Nazi *Wehrmacht*, now in retreat. Hitler was losing his mind thanks to the toxic brews his doctor recommended and his own stress levels. The Allies were gaining the upper hand in southern Europe, where Allied forces had successfully invaded in Sicily and Italy, and in Africa where the Krauts had been rousted. But the Nazis were anything but done. They still held the Western front all the way to the North Sea and the Atlantic coast.

***

While at Camp Ritchie and throughout the war Paul took seriously the imperative for secrecy about the nature of his official activities, and of course all his mail was thoroughly censored. In his frequent correspondence to Margo, he related little of substance, mostly loving husband to loving wife stuff.

And on March 4, 1944, with Paul at Camp Ritchie, Margo gave birth to their first son, named Steven Ernest Mayer, the middle name given in his grandfather's honor. I was born in Manhattan's Wickersham Hospital shortly after Margo and Ida arrived by taxi after attending a play on Broadway. In an enthusiastic style of German journaling, Ida committed these two entries to her daybook: "*Othello/Paul Robeson*" and "*Steven*."

Paul caught a ride in a hearse from Ritchie to New York to inspect his newborn son behind the glass in the hospital, but had to return immediately to resume his training. In his subsequent correspondence to Margo, he expressed his love for her and their son.

He looked forward to getting to know him and raising him in the manner they'd imagined in their intimate moments together. Days later I was brought home to our apartment in Kew Gardens.

"Bye-bye darling, we're on our way"

On April 5, a month after the birth of their darling son, Staff Sergeant Paul A. Mayer received his diploma for "satisfactorily completing the course prescribed for the sixteenth class at the Military Intelligence Training" at Camp Ritchie, hand-stamped #6071.

Paul's Camp Ritchie diploma, April 5, 1944

With his April diploma in hand but still at Ritchie, time passed, with more instruction, field maneuvers, and a good deal of waiting for the opportunity to ship overseas. He and "the boys" knew, unofficially at least, that big preparations for a massive invasion of

Europe were underway in England. The strategic planning and on-the-ground logistics for such an operation were enormous but somehow miraculously kept secret, as countless postwar movies and documentaries describe. The German high command, which was understandably distracted by the rapid unraveling of their glorious leader's vision and sanity, would be caught by surprise.

At some point a Ritchie unit was gathered to ship out, but Paul, who on recent training maneuvers had badly injured his eye and was in the Camp's hospital, couldn't join them. As it happened, the team that was sent were all killed soon after arrival, presumably in those days or weeks after the successful invasion of Normandy.

More waiting.

Newsreel (late 1944)

July 9–British and Canadian troops capture Caen, France.

July 18–U.S. troops reach St. Lô, France.

July 20–Assassination attempt by German Army officers against Hitler fails.

July 24–Soviet troops liberate first concentration camp at Majdanek.

August 1–Polish Home Army uprising against Nazis in Warsaw begins.

August 4–Anne Frank and family arrested by the Gestapo in Amsterdam, Holland.

August 19–Resistance uprising in Paris.

August 19/20–Soviet offensive in the Balkans begins with an attack on Romania.

August 25–Liberation of Paris.

August 29–Slovak uprising begins.

August 31–Soviet troops take Bucharest.

September 1-4–Verdun, Dieppe, Artois, Rouen, Abbeville, Antwerp and Brussels liberated by Allies.

September 13–U.S. troops reach the Siegfried Line in western Germany.

September 17–Operation Market Garden begins (Allied airborne assault to free Holland).

September 19-December 16–Battle of Hürtgen Forest, just inside Germany from Belgium.

September 26–Soviet troops occupy Estonia.

October 10-29–Soviet troops capture Riga.

October 14–Allies liberate Athens; Rommel commits suicide.

October 21–Massive German surrender at Aachen, Germany.

October 30–Last use of gas chambers at Auschwitz.

November 20–French troops drive through the 'Beffort Gap' to reach the Rhine, and four days later capture Strasbourg.

December 16-27–Battle of the Bulge in the Ardennes.

December 17–Waffen-SS murder eighty-one U.S. POWs at Malmedy.

December 27–Soviet troops besiege Budapest.

On July 12, Paul wrote Margo to tell of his address: Psychological Warfare Detachment, Supreme Headquarters Allied Expeditionary Force, under the command of General Dwight D. Eisenhower, in southern England. This greatly pleased Paul. Finally, a destination and some real purpose for Paul, with General Eisenhower at Supreme Headquarters!

"Bye-bye, darling," Paul wrote to Margo on July 19. "I'm on a mission, and I'm looking forward to it," he might well have added. He left the next day, bound for the "European Theater of Operations," the most specific destination he was permitted to name.

On the way over he entered a game of gin-rummy, playing for "ETO stakes," which he claims were never exactly explained to him. It was a long crossing, but he fortunately won big in the last hand of the voyage before learning how close he'd come to losing several months' pay.

He also used the time to study again his Ritchie materials on proper interrogation methods, and to review the goals of the Psychological Warfare Division, which were then to:

- Wage psychological warfare against the enemy
- Use various media to sustain the morale of people of friendly nations occupied by the enemy
- Conduct propaganda directed toward a military force and designed to ensure compliance with the instructions of the commander of the occupying force
- Control information services in Allied-occupied Germany

First stop, "somewhere in England," using the language of Allied censors, approximately five weeks after D-Day ("D" is for the French *Débarquement*), aka Operation Overlord, as it was known to its English-speaking planners working for months and even years in full secret mode.

This landing of allied forces on the Normandy coast on June 6, their first foothold in Europe since the Nazis vanquished all opposition on its Western front two years previously, was probably the most consequential event of the war, at least in the West. With it came the beginning of the end, or the end of the beginning of the end, as Churchill would say.

Five weeks after this landing, July 23, Paul cabled Margo, "All well and safe…" he remained "somewhere in England" as Allied forces continued to advance in France, slowly and painfully making their way towards Paris amidst much battling and taking of German prisoners. Many of these prisoners were taken to England as "customers" (again the secret parlance acceptable to the censors) of the interrogating Ritchie Boys.

"The place where we are now is pretty sinister, but the work seems to be interesting," Paul noted in his first real letter from England, July 27. German troops captured during Operation Overlord as the Allies advanced into Continental Europe were brought to already-constructed POW camps in England where Paul and his team of interrogators were ready for them.

During Paul's time "seeing customers" and "doing business" in the POW camps "somewhere in England," he wrote frequently to Margo, strictly family stuff, noting contacts with friends he was able to meet on leave, or perhaps evenings when he could go "into town" to visit friends they both had known from their year in England just before war broke out.

***

Paul's unit was moved closer to the action, across the Channel to France. On September 14, Paul rode armed and with "his boys" into Paris in their Jeep, barely three short weeks after the German Army surrendered the French capital to the Allies. The German Army was in retreat, and Paul was ready to kick ass and interrogate any fucking Nazi Kraut bastard who stood between him and the rescue of his parents and the surrender of the entire Nazi regime—and bayonet his sorry German-speaking butt if he resisted.

That must have been a moment.

Paul wrote to Margo across the ocean and reminisced about their first months romancing in the Paris Spring of 1933, more than ten years earlier in another time on what must have felt like another planet. It's remarkable to still have these letters, both intimate and mundane, now all part of the Archive at Leo Baeck Institute.

"Remember, darling?" They'd been standing in line at *L'Agence des Droits de l'Hommes,* each wondering if they'd ever be able to go home again. And where he'd introduced himself, *"I think I can help..."* A lot of water under *that* bridge. Paul would write to Margo typically twice a week, always secretive about his "business" activities but alive with quotidian affairs, the constant need for cigarettes and cigars, even months after the Liberation of Paris. And "send candy, candy, candy!" Paul wasn't known for a sweet tooth, but perhaps these were meant to sweeten the conversation with his "customers."

Paul thoroughly masked his movements and purposes in his archived correspondence, allowing himself only to relate stories of acquaintances known to Margo or to his sister Illa. Only one letter from this period shows redactions, where Paul slipped into a revealing attribution, but the censor was on it!

More action. Soon afterwards, Paul reported his assignment as "4th Mobile Radio Broadcasting Company, Signal Corps, Intelligence Section, Psych Warfare Division, SCHAEF." He was apparently in Luxembourg to help erect a huge radio tower to transmit Allied messages ("Lay down your arms! Surrender while you have the chance!") to retreating Germans. He spoke later about sitting around the campfire with these new boys, listening to them make spirited music with their banjos and songs from home. "I knew then that we'd certainly win the war."

He also wrote, "It's freezing, and our only hot water is a helmet full. The food is sometimes OK, sometimes not." But occasionally they're in a nicer place, now some miles outside Paris, with rooms of their own, and blankets, and decent French meals. His unit seemed to move around a lot, with changes in the cast of characters and authority—always vague, dated with "somewhere in France," always approved by a censor.

"Tell me your name, Officer"

In early October, his unit established itself in Compiègne, to the north of Paris, where General Eisenhower had planted his Supreme Headquarters. Compiègne is a place loaded with historic symbolic value. Napoleon had bestowed his wife Eugenie with a very fine *château* there, complete with royal forest and hunting grounds. But more important, it was at Compiègne in 1918 that Germany's military leadership were made to surrender and sign the Armistice that acknowledged their defeat and ended their armed hostilities, in a military railway car on a siding in the former royal forest.

A few years later, the pendulum swung the other way. Hitler was determined to avenge Germany's earlier humiliation, and in June 1940 in Compiègne, following the *Wehrmacht*'s forceful invasion of France, Hitler marched the French President into that same parked railway car and made him sign away French power over France. Humiliation back! It's because of its symbolic significance that General Dwight D. Eisenhower chose Compiègne as the site of the Supreme Headquarters Allied Expeditionary Force.

It was also a good place to interrogate captured *Wehrmacht* officers, and the setting for one of the most pivotal events in Paul's life.

One day in October, a weary and haggard German officer was brought to Sgt. Mayer. Paul instantly recognized him as a long-ago chum from Köln, Anton Comes, a close family friend from grade school, law school, and many a Karnival (aka *Mardi Gras*.) Best of friends for many years. There they were, Paul on one side of the barbed wire barrier in his US Army uniform, and Anton on the other side in his German Army uniform.

Recall that these Ritchie Boys were well-trained in the arts of interrogation, the subtle art that wins trust to get better results than the brutal art inflicted by the US in more recent times. The training at Ritchie was sophisticated, striving to get prisoners to reveal information that's believable and verifiable. They knew how to draw out information from a captured person, playing on trust along with a whiff of threat if cooperation wasn't forthcoming.

The last thing any captured German wanted was to be given

over to the Russian Army, made up of Slavs with a reputation for brutality. The threat of this was held over the prisoners, and it was an effective threat for many. These Germans had been fighting a rearward action for many weeks, pleasant memories of their occupation of Paris now distant in the rear-view mirror. Many were exceptionally young or exceptionally old replacements and had been subjected to the propaganda sent from their own Nazi headquarters. They had no good way of knowing if Russian military was near, but it was a potent threat, nonetheless. Besides, the *Wehrmacht* knew that their retreat from Paris, if it persisted into a full-blown retreat through the winter back into Germany, all the way back to Berlin (which they'd be forced to defend), would be long and torturous.

Anton came from Catholic Köln aristocracy, was himself a lawyer with a promising future if it weren't for this damnable war. Anton was an officer who most likely knew a lot, like key elements of the military's current and rapidly deteriorating capabilities, its plans such as they were in such a chaotic situation, as well as the quality and morale of *Wehrmacht* leadership nearby and all the way to Berlin. He was, as they say in spy novels, a "major asset."

But interrogations didn't always go by the Ritchie training book, and Paul's correspondence reveals there was considerable discussion and controversy among his colleagues about how to handle certain kinds of situations and certain kinds of prisoners, especially those who may have been friends with the interrogator in an earlier life in a more civilized Germany.

Following his interrogation of Anton, Paul insisted his former friend wasn't "a real Nazi." Anton had been forced to join the Party so he could keep his standing as a lawyer. Paul understood this dilemma, having been denied that opportunity himself. Many joined the Party out of convenience rather than conviction. But this reasoning didn't sit well with many of Paul's colleagues who tended to see *all* Germans as Nazis, despite their Ritchie training, especially Germans in uniform near the front. These colleagues made life difficult for Paul.

Paul held his own in these discussions. His position (and he was not alone) was aligned with US Intelligence Service doctrine, that not every German was a Nazi, and not every member of the Nazi party was "a real Nazi"—there could often be extenuating circumstances. Perhaps more important, Paul's job in Intelligence wasn't to punish Nazis—that would come later—but to get information from these prisoners that would expedite the war effort.

Paul kept his powder dry, writing to Margo of barracks discussions of "fairness, justice, and what's the more genuine American way." (One hears echoes of possible consultations with his great-grandfather Samuel.) When some of his Ritchie colleagues reported the disagreement higher up—a "Palace Revolution," as he reported it to Margo—Paul took the high road, insisting this kind of disagreement could be resolved peaceably amongst themselves. He understood where "his boys" were coming from and insisted they're "good boys."

Paul's superiors stood by him, openly appreciating the way he handled himself. In recognition, they selected him for special assignments. Paul enthusiastically related to Margo that he was even now waiting on word for such an assignment, one that would put him in the company of more senior officers.

***

All along the "Watch on the Rhine," as the German leadership came to call it, the German army fiercely resisted the demands to surrender or retreat. It thwarted a largely British expedition to cross the Rhine in the north of Holland (Operation Market Garden, seen in the film, "A Bridge Too Far"). Further south and east of Aachen in Germany just east of Belgium, there was hellacious fighting lasting *three months* in the Hürtgen Forest, a fifty-square mile area that included almost at its center Ernst's former hunting cabin known as Zweifallshammer where just a few years earlier Illa made friends with the corralled boar. Zweifallshammer lay directly on the so-called Siegfried Line of tank defenses that the *Wehrmacht* had constructed to keep the Allies away from a direct approach to the Rhine.

The Germans were desperate to hold on at this defense line and to keep the Allies from breaking through. The *Wehrmacht*, under the control of General Model who had also successfully defended the bridges over the Rhine in the Market Garden operation, prevailed in the *Hürtgenwald* as well, but with extraordinary loss of life on both sides.

Paul, then in France and Luxembourg and perhaps Belgium with "his Ritchie boys," was certainly aware of the Battle of Hürtgen Forest as it was playing out, and it's likely that Illa in Mississippi followed the protracted struggle in newscasts. It's even possible that Ernst in Theresienstadt heard rumors arriving on incoming trains. But they could not have been aware of the human tragedy of up-close warfare playing out on the Zweifallshammer property itself, where bodies were piling up and where those two buildings adjacent Ernst's cabin, those woodland World War I era military field hospitals, were in use again in futile efforts to treat the wounded. In the First World War, German civilization allowed Dr. Mayer to treat the wounded, but thirty years later, as a German Jew, he was stripped of his professional standing and his citizenship, deemed unsuitable to treat the German Christian soldiers of the Master Race, and sent to a damned concentration camp.

The Battle of Hürtgen Forest took the lives of upwards of 55,000 Americans and 28,000 Germans, and was the longest battle fought by US forces in the European Theater, lasting eighty-eight days. The US Army had superiority of numbers, but weather and densely forested terrain worked against US advantages. It became a prolonged, catastrophic defeat, described as an Allied "defeat of the first magnitude."[31] Soon after, the fatigued armies on both sides re-

---

31 Whiting, Charles (1989). *The Battle of Hürtgen Forest*. New York: Orion Books. Also, MacDonald, Charles B. (1984) [1963]. *The Siegfried Line*

grouped and prepared for the next confrontation, known in English as the Battle of the Bulge, a critical and famous battle, also with huge losses under awful winter conditions, but this time the Allies prevailed and re-formed to assault the Rhine River directly.

Mission interruptus, and Paul evacuates

On December 14, a few weeks after interviewing Anton Comes, just as the action moved away from Zweifallshammer to begin the final assault on the Rhine, Paul wrote to his sister in Mississippi from Paris. "I'm suffering a terrible case of GI diarrhea, which makes me stop this letter very abruptly. Must sign off." This sort of news had entered their correspondence before, but this time it was followed by a protracted silence that his family had not experienced.

Weeks later he renewed his letters to Margo and described what had happened.

Just before Christmas 1944, after his last post to Illa, he was working in or near Paris "interviewing customers." On a weekend pass, Paul emerged from a cinema in Montparnasse and collapsed to the sidewalk. He was taken by ambulance to the American Hospital in Neuilly where they did emergency surgery on a "ruptured duodenal ulcer." They saved his life, but barely.

He alluded to this close brush with death later in a telegram from "somewhere in England," to "my darling *Margaretechen*, I'm positively out of danger," followed by more reflective letters acknowledging how lucky he was and how dangerous the situation really was, and how deliriously happy he was now that the awful past was behind him. He could now look forward to beginning a new life with his beautiful and wonderful wife, perhaps after some time in a convalescent facility, perhaps in England, or perhaps in the United States, too early to know.

---

campaign. Center of Military History, United States Army. Quoted in https://en.wikipedia.org/wiki/Battle_of_H%C3%BCrtgen_Forest#CITEREFMacDonald1984

The tone of these "deliriously happy" communications suggests they were morphine-induced, which he later acknowledged. His little endearments and loving sentiments were not new, however. Almost all his letters to Margo from the beginning of his service in the US Army began or ended that way.

From his hospital bed in England, still in grave danger but insisting otherwise, Sgt. Mayer must have felt keen disappointment. He had so wanted to advance into Germany and beyond, all the way to Theresienstadt. He never had the opportunity to fire at the enemy. He never got to use his bayonet to shove with conviction into the guts of those fuckers who had taken his parents and abused and disrespected them as they herded them into those trains carrying them East. He didn't get to serve with "his boys" to take the fight to the Nazis and see the war to its cleansing and healing finish.

What a disappointing end to his forward march into Germany and the fulfillment of his wartime dream. He missed the climax and had to sit it out convalescing in hospitals. Such a shame, in my opinion. The next newsreel reveals what he missed.

Newsreel (1945)

January 1-17–Germans withdraw from the Ardennes.

January 16–US 1st and 3rd Armies link up after a month-long separation during the Battle of the Bulge.

January 26–Soviet troops liberate Auschwitz.

February 4-11–Roosevelt, Churchill, Stalin meet at Yalta to plan how to divvy up Germany and Berlin

March 7–Allies take Cologne and establish a bridge across the Rhine at Remagen.

April 12–Allies liberate Buchenwald and Belsen concentration camps. President Roosevelt dies. Harry Truman becomes President.

April 21—Soviets reach Berlin.

April 28—Mussolini is captured and hanged by Italian partisans; Allies take Venice.

April 30—Adolf Hitler commits suicide.

May 2—German troops in Italy surrender.

May 7—Unconditional surrender of all German forces to Allies.

May 8—V-E (Victory in Europe) Day, the end of the war in Europe.

May 23—SS-Reichsführer Himmler commits suicide; German High Command and Provisional Government imprisoned.

July 1—American, British, and French troops move into Berlin.

August 6—First atomic bomb dropped, on Hiroshima, Japan.

September 2—Japanese sign the surrender agreement; V-J (Victory over Japan) Day.

November 20—Nuremberg war crimes trials begin.

Back in December when he was stricken, the war seemed interminable, and he was filled with worry. It hadn't been that long since he'd learned of his parents' deportation to Theresienstadt, though he hadn't yet learned of their situation after that.

From his hospital bed in England, Paul listened intently to the news. Presumably, his unit had its hands full with new "customers." Many had critical information, and Paul's boys were able to get it.

The Battle of the Bulge was just breaking out to the east of Luxembourg. This battle was the last really big, sustained battle, lasting more than a month with major loss of life but critical to the success of breaking through the Nazi hold on France. The Ritchie Boys are credited with doing a lot to win the war, especially in the Battle of the Bulge, gathering critical intelligence on the order of battle. Who knows how many prisoners Paul had interrogated in those intense months after June when German prisoners were brought to him, first in England and then in France.[32]

Still, he knew by this time that the war was almost as good as won. All the Allied forces on that front were pushing forward as well as they could, and the Nazis were clearly in retreat. There was no place for them to go but "back."

On February 18, 1945, after another six weeks in hospital (six weeks!), Paul wrote "from sea, between the Gulf of Biscayne and the Azores, about four days out" on board the US Military Hospital Ship Chateau-Thierry. At sea, on his hospital ship back to America (a photo of that life-giving ship always hung in his home office), he had plenty of time to ponder his situation. He was gravely injured, still with months of recuperation ahead of him—but he always loved the sea, and the US and its Allies were winning the war in Europe. He was headed home, back to his loving wife and to a son he wanted to get to know and help raise.

MHS Chateau-Thierry, 1945

---

32   Unfortunately, Service records for military personnel, and therefore their units and their units' whereabouts and activities, were destroyed in a major fire in the 1970s, so we may never know

Paul rejoins his family as the war ends

On arrival by US Military Hospital Ship in Charleston, South Carolina on February 28, 1945, Paul was taken by ambulance on a long journey to upstate New York, to Rhoads General Hospital in Utica, where he would then spend *another two months* of convalescence, reflection, and anticipation of a future.

Paul knew little of this future in his still new land, with the prospect of reconstructing the life he was meant to have when the Nazis took away his life's meaning, his citizenship, his right to a livelihood, his rightful inheritance, and his dreams.

In his correspondence with Margo during his convalescence, he was in remarkably good spirits. He was explicitly grateful for surviving a harrowing experience at the very edge, and for this next chapter—very loving, looking forward to a future with his wife whom he very much loved, wishing to spend evenings in their home, watching their son grow up, playing with him, enjoying proper Sunday dinners, standing bravely for the future, working again, maybe as a commercial lawyer in an import/export firm. [Makes me teary. He so wanted the best for us.]

He must have pondered what role his experience with the Ritchie Boys, in Military Intelligence, in the construction of a successful Occupational Government could possibly play in his future… Could he work for the Office of Strategic Services (forerunner to the Central Intelligence Agency)? Could he work in Berlin or Bonn with the Allied Occupational Government? Or in New York with the United Nations?

In late April 1945, the positive resolution of war was in sight, at least in the European Theater of Operations. Already in January, as a most encouraging sign of impending Allied victory, the 1st and 3rd US Armies had linked up and advanced on the Rhine. The Allies bombed the shit out of Köln on my first birthday and took up positions up and down the Ruhr and Rhine River valleys before breaching the Rhine at Remagen in late April and driving (not without resistance, but with definitive momentum) across the German heartland. The race was on to Berlin for the final take-down.

The end for Hitler came when the Supreme Commander and adored Dictator of the Fucking Nazis, in his little underground private bunker beneath Berlin, encircled by the Russian army, chose a drug-induced way out, leaving the "1000-Year Reich" 988 years short of its goal and its capital city above in complete ruin. Russia had taken its revenge (and also, BTW, all of eastern Europe) at Stalin's command, "Show no mercy."

The fate of Paul's parents

As the war was winding down, Paul still didn't know the whereabouts or safety of his parents. This worry continued to eat at him, a worry that certainly delayed the proper healing of the surgical wounds to his stomach.

There had been no word about them since Illa had received news on October 19, 1943 that their parents had been sent to Theresienstadt in June 1942, now almost three years earlier. On July 27, 1945, Paul followed up his sister's request for information, sending a cable to Theresienstadt, asking his parents, "Where and how are you? ... Everything alright here. Baby Steven seventeen months." Finally, on August 30, 1945, in a letter from a friend in Switzerland, Illa's husband Gottlieb was informed of Ernst and Lisbeth's transport to Auschwitz and their immediate death in late October 1944. A few weeks later this news was made official in a letter from Central Tracing Bureau for United Nations Relief and Rehabilitation Administration, Central Headquarters for Germany. So there it was. Official word of the Nazis solving the Jewish problem, the final solution that sent Ernst and Lisbeth up in smoke.

```
                CENTRAL TRACING BUREAU
                       UNRRA
                Central Headquarters for Germany
                APO 757      of     B.A.O.R.        28 SEPT 1946

File: 584-CR (42933/34) T/G/J         No 42933/34

Subject: Report on enquiry concerning missing persons.

To:        G J Marum, MD
           Greenville Miss.
           PO Box 2876
           USA
```
See also Todesbescheinigung

1. Rference is made to enquiry from you, concerning:
Dr. med. MAYER, Ernst, born at Trier, Germany on 25-6-74 and Mrs
Elisabeth MAYER,-Teutschborn 9-1-84 at Metz, Alsace Lorraine,
last known adresses: Koeln 17 Gilbachstr., 80 Sachsenring and
Fort 5. Both deported to Theresienstadt in May 1942.

2. Enquiries based on the information supplied were made,
but it is very much regretted that a report has now been received stating that no trace can be found.
We can inform you that Dr. Ernst Mayer born 25-6-77 has
been deported to Theresienstadt on 16-6-42 Transp. No. 919/III-1
and from there to Auschwitz on 28-10-44, Transp. No. Ev 1073.
Mrs. Elisabeth Mayer also was deported to Theresienstadt on
16-6-42, Transport No 920/III-1, to Auschwitz on 28-10-44,
Transport No. Ev 1072.

3. In view of this the name(s) will be broadcast over
the widest possible radio network, with the request that any per
son who has information will forward it to the Central Tracing
Bureau. Information from a variety of sources is always coming
into this office, and is checked against the register of persons being sought. Any news which comes to hand will be for-
warded to you immediately.
        No further information available.

                            J.R.Bowring
                              Colonel
                    Director, Central Tracing Office Burea

Official Notification of Transportation to Theresienstadt and Auschwitz, Central Tracing Bureau, UNRRA, 1946-9-28

***

How this news was received by Paul and Illa and Margo is unspoken and unknown. With a silent scream, we imagine.

But we now know the sequence of events that led to it. With the Liberation of Paris in August 1944, and the necessary retreat of disorganized and dispirited Nazi forces back eastward, back towards the Rhine, back towards Germany, the Nazis thought it prudent to complete the job on one of their primary missions, the extermination of Europe's Jews.

Somehow, Ernst and Lisbeth had survived the monthly deportations from Theresienstadt to the death camps further east for more than two years, perhaps because Ernst had served the Kaiser as a physician in the Great War, and perhaps because Lisbeth had the needlework skills to teach embroidery to women selected for the Nazi show camp. But now, in October 1944, their time had run out.

Just a few days after Paul confronted his old friend Anton at Compiègne, the Nazi commanders were realizing the Allies were coming and their cause was lost. Hitler ordered Theresienstadt be emptied and its inhabitants shipped to the extermination camp in Poland known as Auschwitz. Ernst and Lisbeth were both loaded onto those cattle cars, like one sees in the movies, and shipped to Auschwitz.

They were among the last to experience the final solution as practiced in Auschwitz, as one final transport of Jews from Theresienstadt, totaling 1,700 men, women, and children, were murdered. The ever-efficient Nazis recorded Ernst's train number 1073, Elizabeth's 1072,[33] on October 28, the last official weekend of extermination operations. When they arrived in Auschwitz the ovens were opened wide to accommodate the last-minute weekend rush as the remains of tens of thousands of expendable Jews shot skyward, their ashes settling wherever the winds carried them.

The proprietors and guardians of the camp cleared out in anticipation of the Allies' ever closer approach.

---

33   Terezin Memorial Museum

The Auschwitz death camp remained open a few months as a holding pen even if no longer a place of industrialized slaughter, and was liberated in January 1945 by a Ukrainian unit of the Red Army approaching from the East.

US General Eisenhower came to the site soon after and insisted that a group of photographers go there and to other death camps to document the atrocities of the Nazis. The photos were to serve as evidence for the people of the world so that there was to be no room for "cynical doubt," as he put it, hopefully.

Here is the photo of Paul's parents, as it hung over his bed every day in his post-war home.

Ernst and Lisbeth, 1938

***

Among the many post-war activities to create real "remembrance" of the war and its costs were several that engaged the Mayer family.

One was the Stolpersteine Project. *Stolpersteine* ("stumbling stones") aim to commemorate individuals at exactly the last place of residency—or, sometimes, work—which was freely chosen by the person before they fell victim to Nazi terror, euthanasia, eugenics, deportation to a concentration or extermination camp, or escaped persecution by emigration or suicide. Initiated by the German artist Gunter Demning in 1992, the Project has coordinated the installation of 75,000 *Stolpersteine* have been laid as of December 2019, making the Stolpersteine project the world's largest decentralized memorial."[34]

"The majority of *Stolpersteine* commemorate Jewish victims of the Holocaust. Others have been placed for Sinti and Romani people (then also called "gypsies"), Poles, homosexuals, the physically or mentally disabled, Jehovah's Witnesses, black people, members of the Communist Party, the Social Democratic Party, and the anti-Nazi Resistance, the Christian opposition (both Protestants and Catholics), Freemasons, International Brigade soldiers in the Spanish Civil War, military deserters, conscientious objectors, escape helpers, capitulators, "habitual criminals," looters, others charged with treason, military disobedience, undermining the Nazi military, and Allied soldiers."

Dr. Ernst Mayer's death along with eleven of his classmates at his Gymnasium in Trier who had met similar fates in Nazi crematoria were commemorated recently through the dedication of a *Stolpersteine* in the courtyard of the church housing their former school on the Jesuitenstrasse.

Stolpersteine **for Dr. Ernst Mayer, Trier, 2022**

---

34 Wikipedia, https://en.wikipedia.org/wiki/Stolpersteine

***

In the Eifel Forest where the Battle of Hürtgenwald created so many casualties, the former *Field Artz* Dr. Ernst Mayer's earlier dedication to civilized medicine lives on in memory at Zweifallshammer. The two rustic clinics on the property was completely overrun with thousands of dead and wounded from the nearby forests and fields, but somehow a young German Army physician from that field hospital (I like to think he'd been a student of Ernst, but the facts don't line up) had enough courage and influence to persuade both the German and American military leadership to call a two-day cease fire so that both sides could attend to the vast numbers of dead and wounded. Apparently he did this more than once, and both German and American soldiers were treated at Zweifallshammer. For his trouble, the Nazis condemned him to death for his treasonous act of using a *Wehrmacht* hospital to treat enemy soldiers, but the war ended before he could be brought to justice. He lived on in obscurity until 1962, but is commemorated at the remarkable volunteer-driven "Museum Hürtgen Forest 1944 and Peacetime."

Book 3: Post-War

The end of the war in 1945 brought great relief and joy to the survivors and victors, however short-lived this joy might be. They at least saw an end to brutal armed conflict. And they could see concerted effort at rebuilding property and lives.

It was a time that peace could emerge.

Newsreel (1945–1947)

1945–End of World War II in Europe and the division of Germany into four occupation zones by the Allied powers.

1945–The United States drops atomic bombs on Hiroshima and Nagasaki, leading to the end of World War II and the beginning of the nuclear age.

1945–Beginning of the Cold War, an extended period of heightened and often hostile tensions between the Soviet Union and the United States, initially over the political map of Eastern Europe following the end of World War II.

1945–Establishment of the United Nations on October 24, aiming to maintain international peace and security.

1945-46–Nuremberg Trials. The prosecution of major war criminals from the Third Reich, which established a legal precedent for dealing with war crimes and crimes against humanity.

1946–Winston Churchill's "Iron Curtain" speech on March 5, highlighting the division between the Soviet Union and the West.

1947–Announcement of the Marshall Plan on June 5, providing economic aid to Western Europe to help rebuild after the war. It's been regarded as one of the most productive foreign policies ever enacted by the US, and laid the groundwork for USAID.

1948–"Benelux," a politico-economic union comprising Belgium, the Netherlands, and Luxembourg, becomes operational as a customs union to promote economic cooperation and integration among the three countries by ensuring the free movement of goods, services, capital, and people. It became a model for the development of the European Economic Community and later the European Union.

Ever-loving Margo

From the time her husband Paul went off to join the US Army in 1942 as a buck private enlisted man, Margo busied herself with the life of an Army wife making it on her own in the New World. Paul cheered and was constantly proud of her.

She wrote to Paul frequently, responding to his frequent letters. There would be several pieces of mail going both ways each week, throughout his sojourn from Camp Dix to Camp Blanding, to Camp Custer, to the Citadel, to the University of Illinois, to Camp Ritchie, to "somewhere in England," to "somewhere in France," and then back to England and back to the US on a hospital ship to an Army hospital in upstate New York.

Always little (or big) endearments, encouragement, and support.

While Paul was forever hot to pursue the war and take it to the Nazis, she would try to cool him with, "Don't get involved in anything too dangerous. Remember that you have a responsibility to me."

When Paul complained to her in their correspondence that his skills weren't getting enough attention from 'the brass' and his pursuit of higher rank was being thwarted, she wrote, "I don't care how many stripes you have, just keep doing the good work you do."

Margo would daily take the subway from their apartment in Kew Gardens in Queens to her job at Highfield Trading Company in midtown Manhattan and would describe to Paul the routines of the day. He had briefly worked there himself, after his time at Winkler and before reporting for Army duty, and knew the people and the work, so they both wrote from that mutual familiarity.

Paul would frequently ask for packages of things he couldn't get at the PX-cigarettes or candy or pens or socks or sweaters or some good German *wurst*. Margo would diligently shop for these, package them and put them in the mail.

Margo was on excellent terms with the owner of Highfield, and he and his wife were great friends to her. He and Margo's mother had known each other in Frankfurt, and he treated her a bit like a daughter. He would take her to lunch, occasionally to the theater, and she would join them at their home on occasional weekends. He had a large network of friends, which he shared with Margo.

Paul and Margo had begun saving for the future from the moment they got off the boat, even while living in their cold-water walkup. Paul was a savvy investor and student of market dynamics, especially in blue chip issues traded on the New York Stock Exchange. And he also understood the markets for the kinds of commodities that Winkler and Highfield traded in. Margo would ask Paul's advice on different commercial transactions coming to her attention at work, and Paul would give it. He would also direct her in the purchase and sale of stock issues they owned together.

The back-and-forth wartime correspondence between Margo and Paul is an interesting mix of an intelligent, sociable, capable woman of standing living a well-grounded and well-nurtured life in her adopted New York—interlaced with the quotidian, hard-working, grunting life of an Army barracks brain striving with all his mighty skills to move his war forward.

So, when Paul was finally discharged from the Army hospital at the end of April 1945, damaged but victorious, he stepped onto a well-prepared stage. He joined his wife, his mother-in-law, and his thirteen-month-old son in the small apartment he and Margo had moved into in May 1941.

Just a few days later, we moved together into a new home in Forest Hills, most likely enabled through the GI Bill (passed in June 1944), a real house with real bedrooms and a separate kitchen and basement and trees and a small yard to play in. A few days after that, Paul went back to work at Highfield. And the following day the Nazis surrendered.

Tortured, Paul turns to the law for justice

For Paul, it was a tortured peace. Even though he was now able to rejoin his family and resettle all together in a perfectly fine home in Queens, this was a period of limbo. It was a time of convalescence from his wounds, an arduous process requiring real grit.

The wounds of war come in many ways—physical, emotional, and mental. When Paul collapsed in the streets of Paris and was rushed into surgery, his wounds, as life-threatening as they were, had none of the glamor of wounds sustained in a frontal attack led by an infantry unit commanded by Captain Paul A. Mayer. No, they were the wounds suffered in surgery intended to save his life from bleeding ulcers. Even before he was evacuated from France and sent to England, sepsis set in, requiring a second emergency operation. In 1950 there were indications that his surgical wounds hadn't healed right, and the surgeons had to go in again. It took months and years of convalescence. A lifetime, one could even say.

The wounds of memory can present a worse horror, born silently but visited upon him and his household. The emotional scars from the knowledge his beloved Germany stole everything of value—and murdered his parents. Fearsome wounds of memory. Add to it the growing recognition that while Paul and his parents had loved Germany, Germany didn't love them back, indeed hated them in the worst ways imaginable, leaving lifelong emotional scars and lifelong sorrow in the psychological home where all humans live.

A plan emerged. As he surely discussed with Margo in their early post-war life in New York, saying, "The Allies have done it right this time; they paid good attention to creating the right conditions for a more lasting peace. We can still get some measure of justice and make the Germans pay for their crimes."

Central to their hopes was the pursuit of restitution and compensation of property and assets stolen by the German regime from the time during Hitler's dictatorship from 1933 to the end of the war. The 1945 Treaty of Surrender assured this, as did provisions written into the new German constitution. People could pursue their claims for restitution with credible evidence, presented through legal channels and protocols that were now being formulated.

Pursuing this plan for restitution and compensation would involve a good deal of work, carving out meaningful time for it. Taking such time would likely come at the price of letting go of other options, like striving to become Chief Legal/Finance Officer in some go-go post-war corporate enterprise in Manhattan, one of the foremost financial and commercial capitals of the world.

But success in that arena would require an American law degree. His German training, based on Napoleonic code-based law would have little value in an American judicial system based on English-like precedent-based law. He pondered going to an American law school, but he was forty years old with a family, and it was not a good time for another time-out.

If Paul thought about re-connecting with the Intelligence Service, or with Office of Strategic Services (forerunner of the Central Intelligence Agency), or with the Military Occupation of Germany, or the newly established United Nations, all possibilities his training and experience certainly prepared him for, we never knew. As for returning to West Germany to work with its government to help create an improved legal and civil infrastructure—something he was indeed interested in and well-suited for, Paul later said Margo would never be willing to "go back," as she was a go forward type. It's also likely that Paul already had his fill of the military-bureaucratic complex.

But the possibility of using his legal skills to pursue restitution through legal means of a life lost, *that* had possibilities. It would not bring back his life in his beloved Germany, and it would not bring back his parents, but it could restore his dignity and contribute to at least the beginnings of a sense of justice.

The victorious powers—the US, Great Britain, and France (but not Russia)-had major interest in how the illegal seizure of property previously owned by German citizens (Jews and all the others forced to leave their possessions) were to be re-distributed. They prepared the legal framework and processes for making meaningful restitution and compensation happen for at least some of Nazi Germany's victims, at least those who had lived in Germany.

The stage was set.

"Use me," said Anton

Paul thought about his old school friend Anton Comes whom he had interrogated "somewhere in France" in October 1944. Those days of interrogation were the last Paul had seen or heard about Anton. Köln had been virtually destroyed by American bombing in March. Was Anton even alive? And what about his wife and three children? At the end of 1946 Paul tried to contact him at his last known address in Köln.

Months later, Paul heard back. A friendship was re-kindled. An unusual friendship, given the circumstances, but an opportunity both Paul and Anton embraced. Anton offered his assistance. "Use me," he said.

Anton emerged from the rubble of their hells endured in the war. Anton's family had suffered grievously towards the end of the war. He and his wife Margaret had lost their first born in one of the bombing raids of Köln, and their home and office, twice. Post-war Köln was a wreck, mostly rubble, and aid for reconstruction was not immediate. Paul and Margo on several occasions sent packages of clothing and food. Anton and Margaret were most grateful. Paul said to him, "this is why we spent twelve years together as friends and schoolmates."

By November 1947, the US Office of Military Government in Germany and the US Department of State had the key documents in place to allow the first phases of legal pursuit of restitution and compensation to proceed.

By then, Anton had made progress in moving his pre-war training in law and his position in society into play with roles allied with Konrad Adenauer, who had been leader of the Catholic Centre Party and Mayor of Köln in the Weimar years. After the war Adenauer became Chancellor of West Germany in 1949 and a strong advocate of Atlantic and European economic and military alliances, credited with leading West Germany out of the past and into a brighter future.

Paul and Anton agreed to work together, a remarkable story of reconciliation. With Anton acting in Köln as informal paralegal (one of the most qualified imaginable), making sure Paul's legal case papers were properly entered and moved through the process, Paul could pursue legal actions from New York. They first went after the least-contestable but highly valuable low-hanging fruit-claims for the value of the homes and property of Ernst and Lisbeth, of Margo's mother Ida Kahn Koch Netter, and Paul's sister Illa and her Marum in-laws.

This effort proved fruitful, and Paul then moved beyond the easier pickings to more challenging ones, such as compensation for earnings lost by the deprivation by theft of citizenship or professional licensure. He now could make claims for assets and earnings lost by his father, himself, his sister and her husband, his mother-in-law, and Paul himself (robbed of his career in law).

This kind of reparations work was ground-breaking in the global history of rule by law. Work by the courts in Germany was closely watched. Their declarations, rulings, and protocols set the precedent and stage for reparations that could be pursued by other groups around the world. The genocide of the Jews of Europe isn't the only genocide that's been suffered, but it's the only one, to my knowledge, for which an orderly process of restitution has been mandated and thoroughly pursued.

We can all be thankful the Allies drew on the skills of capable civil servants and lawyers that knew how to write demands of justice and restitution into the fibers of Germany's new constitution and institutions of governance. Lawyers like Paul, in fact, whose work in the US Army was born and rooted in the same sensibility.

More immediately, Paul now had an avenue to do what he needed to do. Providing such an avenue, as the forces of Allied Occupational Government did, is itself a form of justice, allowing him to be that German lawyer after all, fighting to restore [part of] what had been stolen from him and his wife and their extended families. And this role allowed him to relate to the new Germany, built on better sensibilities and values he knew well. It's likely he again heard the voice of Opa Teutsch and his great-grandfather, the lawyer-rabbi Samuel Mayer, whose 1830s likeness now hung by Paul's doorway.

Acculturation as new Americans

Viewers of newsreels and readers of newspapers could already see the beginnings of the next era of international conflict, the so-called Cold War, tinged with the threat of mutually assured mass destruction. There's just no end to the seemingly persistent and increasingly dangerous cycles of violence, when a sense of justice collides with a sense of injustice, the fight is ongoing, and the beat goes on.

Newsreel 1948-49

1948–Adoption of the "Universal Declaration of Human Rights" by the United Nations General Assembly, setting out fundamental human rights to be universally protected, drafted by representatives from different legal and cultural backgrounds from all regions of the world.

1948-1949–The Berlin Blockade and Airlift, where the Soviet Union blocked access to West Berlin, and the Western Allies responded with a massive airlift to supply the city.

1949–Establishment of the Federal Republic of Germany (West Germany) on May 23, and the German Democratic Republic (East Germany) on October 7, with Konrad Adenauer as Chancellor.

1949–Formation of the North Atlantic Treaty Organization (NATO) on April 4, a military alliance between North American and European countries.

***

Paul and Margo's second son Franklin Robert Mayer was born on May 20, 1949. The name Franklin was chosen in grateful acknowledgment of Franklin Delano Roosevelt. If Franklin had emerged as a girl, she would surely have been named Eleanor, widely seen as more pro-semitic than her husband or his State Department. The middle name Robert was chosen by Margo in acknowledgment of her grandfather, the jeweler Robert Koch.

These were the years of my earliest schooling. I remember every room of the house, especially my bedroom with the leafy tree just outside the window, and the chair Margo read to me. Early reads: "*My Father's Dragon*," by Margo's cousin Peter Kahn's wife, Ruth Stiles Gannett, which went on to win several awards, be one of the best-selling children's books of all time, translated into several languages, and the subject of animated and acted films.

And "*Struwwelpeter*," Paul's choice of literature for a child's education, read to his sons in German. Written in 1854 by Heinrich Hoffmann, a Frankfurt physician, "the book relates in highly graphic verse and pictures the often-gruesome consequences that befall children who torment animals, play with matches, suck their thumbs, refuse to eat, fidget at meals, refuse to obey, etc."[35] The book terrorized generations of German toddlers being read to by their fathers. It could be a reason why I refused to learn German.

Paul, still sportive by disposition and a cup-winning tennis player in Köln before the war, wanted to join the nearby Forest Hills Lawn Tennis Association, already the site of the US Tennis Open, to watch if not to play. But again, "No Jews allowed." Another disappointment to bear silently. That government-supported restriction against Jews lived on until the 1964 Civil Rights Act.

In 1950 Paul traveled to Europe for the first time since the war on an extensive evidence-gathering mission to all the key places. But first he needed additional surgery. He'd almost died twice in 1944 and '45, and the surgery left internal scarring that interfered greatly with normal digestion. Poor guy had stomach issues all his life, even before his wartime ulcers, and forever after. Would he have the stamina to travel right after this surgery? Yes, he learned to prevail in the Army, he always said. In fact, I never heard him claim fatigue as an excuse to avoid work.

When Paul returned from his foray to Europe, he wanted to shift his energies to work more on restitution cases. This pursuit would be made easier if he had a more secure and stress-free day job from which he could return at a decent hour and devote evenings to his law practice.

So, he took the advice offered by an occupational therapist at the Veterans Administration during his most recent abdominal repair work and applied for a position with the US Government in Wash-

---

35 "*Struwwelpeter in English Translation (Dover Children's Classics) Paperback*–April 7, 1995, by Heinrich Hoffmann (Author)

ington DC. He succeeded in getting a position with the Department of Commerce, Office of Foreign Trade, European Division.

"Washington should be interesting," thought Paul. "It's not New York and not a major financial capital, but Washington is indisputably the political capital of the free world." Taking this position in Washington required a big move for Paul and his family. It meant leaving the relative familiarity of New York for the hinterland. It meant leaving the once-imagined future as the chief legal officer in some kind of commercial firm. It also meant leaving Illa, who had left Mississippi for New York after being widowed just after the war. It also meant leaving Margo's brother Robert and his new family which had also settled in New York.

So, another leaving, and a big one. This time, at least, the move was not driven by desperation. This time, a more settled, normal life could be foreseen.

Newsreel 1950-1957

1950-1953—Korean War, a proxy war between the U.S.-led United Nations forces and North Korean and Chinese forces.

1951—Formation of the European Coal and Steel Community, where France, West Germany, Italy, Belgium, the Netherlands, and Luxembourg created a common market for coal and steel to bind their economies together.

1952 and 1956—Dwight D. Eisenhower, five-star general and former leader of Allied forces in Europe, elected US President.

1952—West Germany signed the Luxembourg Agreement with Israel, providing material compensation and an official apology for the Holocaust.

1953–The Cuban Revolution begins, led by Fidel Castro.

1954–Following defeat at Dien Bien Phu, France withdraws from Indochina, leaving four independent states: Cambodia, Laos, and what became North Vietnam and South Vietnam.

1954–The Supreme Court rules in Brown v. Board of Education, declaring racial segregation in public schools unconstitutional.

1955–Rosa Parks is arrested for refusing to give up her seat on a bus in Montgomery, Alabama, leading to the Montgomery Bus Boycott.

1955–The Allies end the military occupation of West Germany. The US begins formal diplomatic relations with West Germany, followed soon after by the United Kingdom and France.

1957–The Eisenhower Doctrine commits the United States to defending Iran, Pakistan, and Afghanistan from Communist influence.

1957–The Treaty of Rome establishes the European Economic Community (EEC), aka The Common Market. The founding members were France, West Germany, Italy, the Netherlands, Belgium, and Luxembourg. The EEC aims to create a unified economic area by promoting the free movement of goods, services, people, and capital among member states.

In May 1951, Paul moved his family from New York to Wheaton, a far suburb of Washington, DC, in Montgomery County, Maryland. They drove to Washington in the family's 1947 Oldsmobile to its new home on a barren little street of a half-dozen extremely modest brick homes in the so-called Wheaton Triangle. Georgia Avenue was still two lanes with one or two traffic lights, horses occasionally pastured up to the roadway, and even a blacksmith's workplace nearby. In memory, the setting was bucolic verging on early 1950s "edge city," with five or six single family brick homes in our view.

Next door to us lived two boys roughly my age. Paul witnessed one of them approach me and call me a "dirty kike." Paul instructed me to hit him, which I did with little conviction or understanding but with enough force to send this kid back to his mama, crying. It was maybe the last time I hit anyone but it was memorable.

Paul's office downtown at the US Department of Commerce required a very long bus ride, an hour and a half each way. On his return, after dinner, he would retire to his sweltering attic office to pound his typewriter in the pursuit of some modicum of justice for his family and himself.

The home in Wheaton, it turns out, was in the middle of an area recently zoned for commercial development that brought widened roadways and cleared a forest where we neighborhood kids had unearthed a colonial era "corduroy road" built of logs, to create a formidable shopping mall known as Wheaton Plaza. It's possible Paul had known of this prospect even when he bought that home, hoping to reap the reward of rising property values. But maybe not, as Paul was no speculator.

After two years in the exurbs of Washington, in Spring of 1953, Paul moved the family much closer in, to a nice home in a leafy and established neighborhood just outside the District of Columbia called Chevy Chase, Maryland. This was the less famous edge of Chevy Chase, not one of the toney properties alongside the prestigious private golf clubs (which were still years away from admitting Jews).

It was the first address, 4627 Hunt Avenue, since Paul and Margo were married that Paul could feel proud of. It was a very pleasant home from 1954 through 1963, important family years for the first generation of American Mayers. The two boys shared a bedroom, Ida (my "Omi") had her own room, Margo and Paul had their own bathroom, there was a guest room most often used by Illa when she'd visit from New York, and a scary basement used by Frank and me to create a small woodworking shop and a nifty HO-gauge model railroad.

Margo's constitution was to thrive, and she spread her essential congeniality to others. She was loved by many. Paul loved to gift her, he had a fine sense of what would look good on her, and he loved to compliment her in front of others. He was always proud of her, as first shown in a letter he wrote soon after they arrived in New York in which he gushed about her newly acquired office telephone switchboard skills.

When they could better afford it, he loved to take her (and often the boys) out to dinner. And when Paul largely retired from restitution work, he and Margo traveled together, most frequently to Paris, Frankfurt, and Köln. He was never keen, though, to go to Washington's theater or symphony, just as he felt earlier in Berlin, but "I can still conduct *Eine Kleine Nachtmusik* in my sleep, I heard it so often as a child."

Life had a domestic rhythm to it, a rhythm to the '50s beat of Ozzie and Harriet. The family had breakfast together, and then Paul headed off with his leather briefcase down the street to catch the bus to ride in to the US Department of Commerce, located downtown in the Federal Triangle, practically the geographic center of American governance, in view of the Washington Monument, the Capitol, and the White House. We kids walked to school or took a school bus to Montgomery County schools. Margo had a ten-to-two job continuing her one-woman role ("Gal Friday," as it was known in the 1950s and '60s) so she'd be home by the time we kids returned from school. My Omi was also at home to help with lunch in the early years, as she could manage a can of ravioli for me and my pal Donnie.

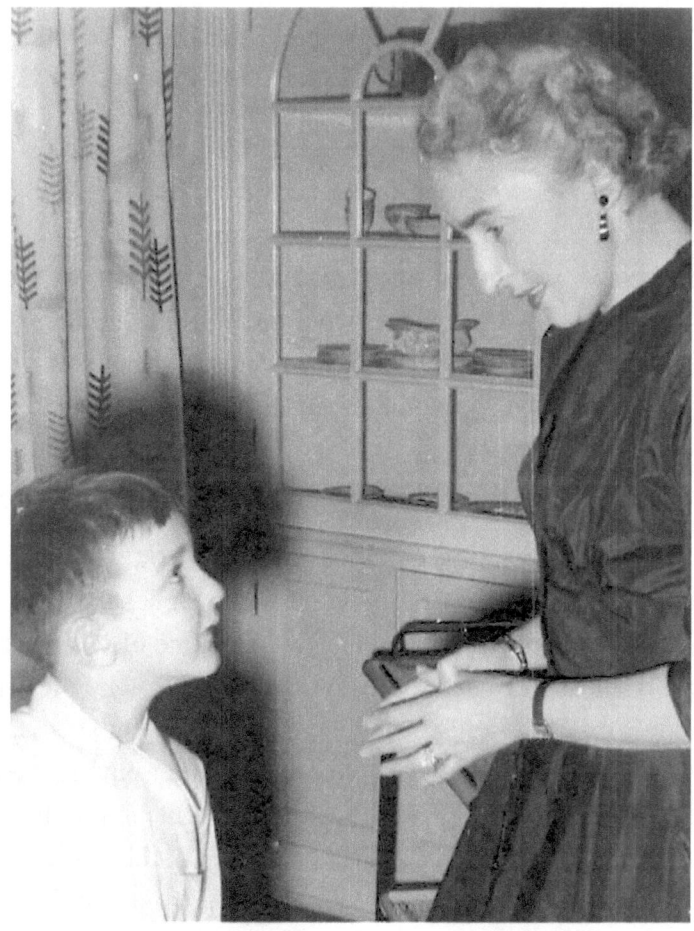

Franklin Robert Mayer, age seven, with Mother (and Koch earrings)

Sunday was also family time. Paul would watch with dismay as I spread the comics and sports pages out on the floor. He and Ida would each do their own New York Times crossword puzzles, in English of course, their third language, Paul using a pen. They would often invite guests for Sunday midday dinner. Sometimes it was a colleague of Paul's at Commerce, or friends visiting from New York, or old friends from Frankfurt or Köln. But visitors or not, the Sunday midday meal was always special. Margo was an excellent cook and had an eye for a promising recipe. Sunday dinner was allegedly a time for talk, about what, I'm still astounded to say, I have no recollection.

This home did not have a dedicated home office, so Paul created a little working niche among the brick and board book shelving in the dining room where he could put his typewriter. Illa shipped him her large Black Forest *armoire* to house his files, which was built in the 1850s and had been a wedding gift but now was less useful to her. After dinner Paul would settle into his home office in the dining room. His ability to concentrate for hours amidst the family din and the heat of summer was astounding. "Learned in the barracks," he always said.

***

Paul's relationship with the Commerce Department was convenient and cordial. He enjoyed working with his colleagues from the European Section of the Foreign Trade Division, some of whom became life-long friends. But just like in the Army, his low-key leadership skills didn't match his talents, and he had difficulty advancing.

His position there was short lived. Soon after buying their nice Chevy Chase home, Paul took a hit. This time he and thousands of others were put in limbo through Federal legislation (the Whitten amendment to the Supplemental Appropriation Act of 1951) that called for a RIF ("Reduction in Force"), a furlough allegedly of indefinite period enacted largely to slow the substantial growth of the Federal Government and the costs that go with it.

So Paul was cut loose again. So much for the job security allegedly attached to employment in the US Civil Service.

During 1953, without steady employment but with a demanding mortgage, Paul worked a few different part-time consulting jobs, as with the Conference Board. Per a résumé written later, he "worked as economic consultant, mainly de-blocking foreign accounts of US nations in European countries, an activity which required mainly knowledge of currency and exchange regulations and the mechanics of international agreements."

This is the one time I saw Margo in tears. Just when they'd moved to what seemed like the just-right place in the just-right time, the future evaporated. "We just can't go on like this."

In May of 1954, Paul traveled to Germany, Paris, and Brussels for three months, partly related to Conference Board assignments, but also to forage for records he could use to pursue his legal claims. While not particularly useful, he somehow unearthed his old school report cards from the rubble of heavily bombed Köln.

In 1955, Congress saw fit to discontinue the RIF and Paul was permitted to re-join the Department of Commerce, but not the European Section of the Foreign Trade Division. Instead, he was placed in the Far East Section. Makes sense, right? He's fluent in German, scores higher in French than anyone since the infamous spy Alger Hiss (he claimed), and does the Sunday New York Times crossword puzzle in ink. Where else but the Far East Division, where none of his three languages is spoken? And he's forced to re-enter at an even lower Civil Service grade level than he'd initially entered. Poor guy can't catch a break. Even the Army did a better job recognizing his talents.

But it still enabled him to leave work at 5pm and come home to join his family for dinner and then head for the old typewriter. The whole house sweltered in the summertime with temperatures and humidity both above 90F for days on end, outside and inside. Paul's daytime office building, the principal building of the US Department of Commerce, was built in 1932 and was entirely without air conditioning, but he never complained. A few years later, with more restitution money available to his family, Paul hired a carpenter to replace the brick and board bookshelves with built-ins and to finish the entire attic to include office space and by this time a dozen file cabinets—and an air conditioner.

But Commerce was just his day job. It provided a rhythm to his day and security for his family. His real work still was the pursuit of restitution after dinner, in the attic. My earliest images of Paul hunched over his typewriter endure, imprinted during my toddler days, persisted over different household moves, into my adolescence and adulthood, until the day he died. Actually, even longer.

Once he was satisfied that he'd achieved as much restitution for his family as was possible, he advised others whom he wanted to help, gaining a reputation as one of the leading restitution lawyers in the country. When the windows of further opportunity were closed by statutes of limitations (in 1969), he turned to curating his files.

Newsreel 1960-1969

1960–Sen. John F. Kennedy, Jr elected President of the US. In 1963, he's killed by assassination.

1961–Construction of the Berlin Wall, which divided East and West Berlin until 1989.

1962–Cuban Missile Crisis from October 16 to October 28, a significant Cold War confrontation involving the U.S., the Soviet Union, and Cuba.

1963–The first major U.S. protest against the Vietnam War was organized by the War Resisters League in New York City.

1963–The March on Washington for Jobs and Freedom, where Martin Luther King Jr. delivers his "I Have a Dream" speech.

1964–Bob Dylan sings, "For the times they are a-changing."

1964–Under President Lyndon Johnson, the Civil Rights Act of 1964 is signed into law, prohibiting discrimination based on race, color, religion, sex, or national origin.

1965–The Voting Rights Act of 1965 is signed into law,

aimed at overcoming legal barriers that prevented African Americans from exercising their right to vote.

1968—The Civil Rights Act of 1968 (also known as the Fair Housing Act) is signed into law, prohibiting discrimination in the sale, rental, and financing of housing.

1969—The Stonewall Riots in New York City mark the beginning of the modern LGBTQ+ rights movement.

Paul had a tenuous and ambivalent relationship with America. He didn't fully belong, he sensed, and didn't really fit in, though one could occasionally see a flash of affection for Americana and its people. He had only to remember "his boys" around the campfire making music to bring that feeling back.

Paul's original connection to America ran through his grandfather's service to the Union Army during the Civil War. At some point in the 1950s, Paul learned that veterans of Adolf's regiment had created a veterans' association, by now maintained by their descendants. Paul joined, thoroughly read its periodic newsletters, and attended at least one of its annual meetings. In later years, he displayed an American flag on the Fourth of July, allowing himself some heartfelt but unspoken sentiment. The American flag was acquired at one of their meetings.

Paul was essentially a patriotic person, patriotic in the sense of felt kinship rather than nationalistic or territorial aspirations. The Vietnam War really tore him up. He wanted his government to be right, but he knew it wasn't. He quietly conspired with the antiwar movement by giving shelter to Margo's cousin Peter Kahn and his students down from Cornell to protest at the big rallies on the Washington Mall.

The civil rights struggle of the 1960s also pulled at his heart strings. One big reason American Jews are so sympathetic to that cause (and active in the fight for civil, human, and equal rights) is our own recognition from our own history of oppression—the myths of racial superiority, the obscene cruelty of still-prevailing Jim Crow laws, and the visual evidence we saw on nightly TV of beatings and intimidation, people stripped of their dignity and humanity. It's no coincidence that so many "Negro spirituals" are inspired by Old Testament stories of Exodus from the land of the oppressive Egyptian Pharoah (like, "Go Down, Moses" or "Joshua Fit the Battle of Jericho.")

***

Over the years, I would tell the family history story to friends, stressing the pivotal parts where the Nazis bar Paul from his profession on the very day he's allowed to enter it. I'd be asked, "So your father never actually was a lawyer?" "Yes, he was," I finally learned to say. "He was barred from courtroom practice in Germany, but he constantly practiced it in the US."

His work life in America was all about lawyering: his work just before and after the war with import/export firms, his time in the Army as a barracks lawyer, as an MP, as political science student at the University of Illinois conjuring a decent German legal system under the rule of a decent civil government, and interrogating captured German POWs with the Ritchie Boys in the European Theater of Operations.

Each of his different positions at Commerce required a good understanding of international commercial law, the field he'd originally trained in. Life in Washington is a paradise for anyone trained in law and political science, fields highly infused with economics, justice, ethics, and journalism.

Paul quickly came to enjoy working the Far East beat, which involved facilitating the US government's trade relations with Thailand, Burma, Borneo, Sarawak, and parts of Indonesia (Vietnam was included elsewhere). He was able to travel there, appreciated what he learned, and wrote a significant publication on trade relations with Thailand. In one of the best photos of Margo in this period she's wearing a spectacular Thai silk dress made for her. He loved that dress, and her in it—and especially out of it (I was told).

Margo and Paul in Thai silk dress, ca 1964

A few years later Paul was transferred within Commerce to a unit organizing "trade fairs," contemporary versions of those fairs held in Europe since medieval times. The Frankfurt Fair, for example, goes back to 1240, making it the oldest in Europe. Hopefully, the book you are reading this very moment will be presented at its world-famous Frankfurt Book Fair, held on those ancient fairgrounds (which, by the way, can almost be seen from my mother's former window in Frankfurt's West End neighborhood). The intention of such fairs, then and now, is to stimulate commerce between regions and industries, a tradition living on now in America where virtually every state has an annual state fair, with similar purposes as in days of yore. One of Paul's more memorable experiences involved him shepherding a group of German cattle ranchers around Utah, introducing conversations with potential buyers. Wearing a formidable western sheepskin coat from Shepler's, he enjoyed it.

Newsreel 1967-1971

Protests against the Vietnam War were a significant part of the antiwar movement in the United States and around the world. Here are some key events:

1967–The March on the Pentagon, where around 100,000 protesters gathered at the Lincoln Memorial, with 30,000 continuing to the Pentagon.

1968–The Tet Offensive in Vietnam marks a turning point in U.S. involvement in the Vietnam War.

1968–The Democratic National Convention in Chicago saw massive protests and clashes with police.

1969–The Moratorium to End the War in Vietnam, a series of massive demonstrations across the United States.

1970–The Kent State shootings, where National Guardsmen shot and killed four students during a protest at Kent State University.

1971–The May Day protests in Washington, D.C., where thousands of protesters attempted to shut down the government.

***

In the early 1970s, when Paul's restitution work was essentially complete, Paul began to exercise his creative brain in new ways.

He began an affiliation with *Aufbau* ("Reconstruction"), a German-language monthly newspaper published in New York. First

My Father Against the Nazis

writing short Letters to the Editor, he then created a role for himself as contributing writer, but because his daytime employer was the US Federal Government, he needed a pseudonym. He chose "Cassandrus."

Cassandra, in Greek mythology, was a daughter of Trojan nobility and a priestess of Apollo. She was cursed with the ability to proclaim true prophecies of the future but never to be taken seriously. In modern usage her name is used to indicate someone whose accurate prophecies are not believed.

It was a perfect pseudonym for Paul, this prophet who was never to be taken seriously. Paul first took on this role in England, when he tried to warn the Brits in true prophetic style, "The Krauts are coming! The Krauts are coming!" but to no avail. "Why should we believe you?" they responded.

Using this pseudonym gave Paul cover, and he used it to write on several subjects, publishing until 1980. He wrote on subjects relating to international affairs and US politics, including an interview with Walter Mondale, then a presidential aspirant.

Several drafts on other subjects were turned down by the Editor as unnecessarily provocative, despite their truth-telling and despite the deniability one wants from such a pseudonym.

In one, he relates how as a soldier recuperating in an Army hospital in upstate New York, listening on the radio to the Allies' race to Berlin to finish the Nazi regime, he exhorted the Allies to advance all the way to Moscow to nip the ambitious Soviet Republic's Stalinist regime in the bud before it could seize control of all of Eastern Europe and potentially further west.

In another opinion piece, also not published, he warned against the excesses of an ambitious nationalist State of Israel. "Thinking that you own land means you have to think of defending it against others, which typically requires a lot of resources and distracts you from more productive and meaningful ways of thinking," is how he spoke of his problem with Zionism.

***

In the years that Paul worked at the Commerce Department, he took his midday meal "out," walking to the nearby commercial area of downtown DC. He was a restaurant guy, and was particularly fond of Costin's Steak House, Blackie's House of Beef, and the National Press Club.

Paul was admitted to the National Press Club using his credentials as correspondent with *Aufbau,* the monthly newspaper to which he contributed. Paul enjoyed the Press Club's facilities, especially its very clubby reading room, bar, and restaurant, just up the street from Commerce.

Membership gave him access to the live weekly noontime Press Club radio presentations that were broadcast across the nation. These programs featured interviews with celebrity Washington pundits and officials who spoke on all manner of current events, conducted in the comfortable setting of the mostly friendly Press Club. Paul enjoyed the intimate setting and staying abreast in this way as an insider, appreciating the social political views of American life expressed there.

On those rare days when school would be off, he would invite me along, first taking me upstairs to his office to meet his current colleagues, then down to the lobby that housed the National Aquarium to visit its prized two-headed turtle, then to check the progress of the Census Bureau's huge population ticker, and then out for lessons in restaurant comportment and how to order the just-right martini.

***

Occasionally, there would be the whiff of the awful past. Someone at a neighborhood gathering in our leafy suburb outside Washington, DC would tell an anti-Semitic joke-nothing really bad, just your basic guffaw-type joke drawing on common stereotypes, but told with the intent to get a reaction. My mother would conceal her sense of dread, but my father would respond right back with his own joke.

He'd laugh and the neighbors would laugh and keep up the mood of the party.

He had a real smile, and though his laugh was quiet, he had a genuine sense of humor. One evening, while watching the evening news at home with his sons, a story about the world's overpopulation came on. Cronkite said, "Every second, somewhere around the world, there's a woman giving birth." And Paul said, "Well, they should just find that woman and stop her." That's a humor born in a fine understanding of the intricacies of the English language. He was not above penciling corrections into books just purchased, restaurant menus, and his sons' student papers. He was also fond of The Three Stooges and all forms of low humor, especially limericks. Go figure.

Always quietly class-conscious, Paul enjoyed those moments when he could exchange pleasantries with, say, the taxi driver, or the bartender. Or at home, he would entice the carpenter away from his bookshelf construction with a martini at the end of the day.

***

Living with Ida, my Omi (the familiar and endearing German term for Oma or Grandmother), was a most wonderful special treat, appreciated especially in hindsight. She was my real link to our European past. We were close and would have actual conversations, and she was actually interested in me and treated me as if I were a real person.

By this time, she had an astonishing résumé of interesting and unusual day jobs, especially for a woman of her standing, a record she began on arrival in England in 1938. Though she'd never learned to cook or clean, having been raised with household staff, she was not reluctant to work. Her visa to Great Britain permitted her employment, and she was hired by retail department stores, nice ones, typically at the handkerchief counter. She continued this in New York and Washington as well. As an elegant, soft-spoken, dignified but egalitarian lady, she sold many fine handkerchiefs, and enjoyed her work.

My Omi, Ida Kahn Koch Netter, 1964

Then she tried her hand selling Childcraft and World Book encyclopedias, not door-to-door, but pursuing leads given her by management. She became famous throughout the Washington DC area as a closer, good with customers who needed a last gentle tug from an educated stylish woman with a pleasant English German accent.

In 1960, when she was seventy, she finally moved out to an apartment of her own. Even though she and Paul, her son-in-law, had a perfectly agreeable relationship and had lived together for almost twenty years, Paul and Margo (I wasn't consulted) apparently decided it was time for some separation, and she could now afford it. Then with vision loss and increasing confusion, she first took in a companion and eventually moved to a nursing home. When she had a stroke, I returned from my home in Minneapolis and climbed over the bed rail and onto her bed where we shared sweet unintelligible conversation set on a boat travelling along the Rhine. My Omi.

***

Margo still maintained her part-time day job,

But her interests expanded, and when invited by a friend to try her hand at teaching German in the Montgomery County Adult Education Program, she accepted. She found she was a good teacher, partly because she was so relatable personally, and partly because she understood the German language as something that could be taught.

A few years later, still during the Cold War, Margo was recruited by an organization known variously as "the Chamber of Commerce," "Langley," "the building next to the Virginia Department of Transportation's Storage Facility," or when the dust settled, the Central Intelligence Agency.

She was hired to teach German to the State Department's Foreign Service personnel bound for German-speaking lands: West and East Germany, Austria, Switzerland, Belgium, Luxembourg, and Lichtenstein. "The Agency"—yes, that's what the CIA is called in DC and Netflix movies—recognized her teaching talent and sent her to a training program in Germany to update her 1930s vocabulary, and then to US Navy's Monterey Language School, the Government's premier school for teaching foreign language skills.

Margo served for ten years as a parttime instructor, conducted regular immersion weekends for students of all levels of skill, and was part of the "German proficiency testing team." She loved it all and was pleased to "give back" to the country that had helped give her and her husband a new life, that's how she put it. Paul was extremely proud of her. In 1990, she retired to great acclaim.

***

Other than his sister, Paul had no close relatives in the United States. He had first cousins on his mother's side in Belgium, Switzerland, and Germany whom he rarely saw, and one on his father's side in Washington DC he saw once every few years, usually when Illa was in town. Paul also had a number of second and third cousins in America, all from his mother's Teutsch side, but they had emigrated two generations earlier and were unknown to him.

There were, however, plenty of Margo's kin in the US, the Kochs and Kahns, and we were all quite close, even when we lived pretty far apart. Once they were properly landed and settled in this country and had securely established themselves with healthy and meaningful lives, we visited frequently, in varying combinations and permutations—and still do.

Paul was of course included, welcomed, and respected in this clan of Kochs and Kahns, and he appreciated every one of them. He couldn't be closer to the Kochs, as his mother-in-law lived under the same roof for almost twenty years, and his two brothers-in-law Robert and Eric were almost annual visitors to their mother, coming from Los Angeles and Toronto.

***

The acculturation of the two sons into their Jewish heritage was something Paul and Margo took seriously, but not very. They were dutiful but not enthusiastic, probably the same as their own parents—"cultural Jews, not religious Jews," as today's meme would say. The Sabbath was not observed as anything special. The family observed the High Holidays by going to services, and they hosted a Passover Seder on one or two occasions for their children's education. They also lit candles for Hannukah, but gift giving was reserved for Christmas. Paul had grown up with a Christmas tree and took great pleasure in providing and decorating one each and every year.

Paul did not insist or even suggest his sons undertake the rigors of the *bar mitzvah* ritual. He did insist, however, that his family be members of a Reformed Jewish congregation, that his sons attend "Sunday school" through tenth grade when they would also take extra classes with the rabbi and be required to attend ten sabbath services during that year. Then they were pronounced "confirmed" in a group ceremony. Somehow picking up on my father's general antipathy to organized religion, I disliked Sunday School, but liked my confirmation rabbi, Leon Adler of Temple Emannuel in Kensington, Maryland. Years later, after a chance encounter, he told me, "You shoulda been a rabbi." This took me aback, but I've marveled at it ever since.

Paul himself wanted no part of synagogue life beyond official membership, and the family changed synagogues frequently. The problem? Paul really objected to institutional Judaism's increasing embrace of Zionism. In post-War America, in the wake of the creation of the State of Israel, Paul thought Judaism, even Reform Judaism, had become too Zionist. It pained him to see this development, as he associated it with nationalism and militarism, and he really didn't want to be part of it. "Becoming a nation state with its claim to land ownership and borders to defend or expand invites trouble," he said more than once.

***

Using her World Book connections, my Omi found a summer camp, called Camp Catawba, that Paul and Margo thought entirely suitable for me at ages eight, nine, and ten, and later for Frank as well. The director, Dr. Vera Lachman, had been a prominent educator in Berlin, and after fleeing Germany took a position as Professor of Classics at Brooklyn College in New York. In the early 1950s, just a few years after the war ended, she created a camp for kids, all the still poorish children of German Jewish refugees.

The camp was in the beautiful Blue Ridge Mountains of North Carolina, first at Black Mountain where there were other camps famous for welcoming the children and parents of northern libs and intellectuals, and then near Blowing Rock, adjacent to the Moses Cone estate.

There weren't many kids, maybe thirty-five, separated by age into six bunk rooms in "the Citadel," a ramshackle wooden building always about to collapse into the hillside. But the culture of the place was straight out of Weimar, a "culture camp," spanning all of July and August. In the evening, Vera would gather all the campers around the campfire and tell stories from the Iliad, Odyssey, and Aeneid—one entire epic each of the three years I went. Most prominently, at the end of the year, we enacted a Greek play by Aristophanes, Sophocles, or Euripides. Paul and Margo drove down the newly constructed Blue Ridge Parkway, dodging hotels that wouldn't admit Jews, for the final weekend of camp to see the play we'd worked on for weeks, which few of us understood.[36]

**

In 1963, Paul moved the family further out from Chevy Chase into the land of three-quarter acre lots and country clubs, to outer Bethesda. This house on Meadowlark Lane was Paul's dream house. Finally, he had a home he clearly enjoyed, with its fireplace, large, screened porch embedded in the surrounding stand of oak trees. He loved that. And not having to mow the lawn himself or even rake the leaves. Finally, a bit of the good life.

Margo, who inherited her mother's discomfort with displays of wealth, was initially reluctant to make this move. But they struck a deal, and Paul purchased a piano so that his lovely wife could again play after almost forty years, complete with lessons from the very accomplished pianist next door. She also found space to garden to her heart's content.

Paul had a spare bedroom converted into his home office, and hired his bookshelf carpenter to make built-in cabinets, including

---

36   See Charles A. Miller, *A Catawba Assembly*, Trackaday, 1973.

an outsized one to house his complete collection of New Yorker magazines.

***

While still on Hunt Avenue, Paul had healed enough from his wartime wounds to play the occasional game of tennis. He began with the public park courts in Chevy Chase, playing with Commerce buddies, Clarence and Fred.

After moving to Meadowlark Lane, he still had game, and remembering the rebuff handed him by the Forest Hills Tennis Club, he became a founding member of Lakewood Country Club, which thanks to the newly enacted Civil Rights Act of 1964 had no membership restrictions in policy or practice as to race, color, sex, religion, or national origin.

Paul didn't play golf, but the club's tennis courts were a draw, and he always wanted to be part of a club. He played until he hurt his back badly while going down for a low backhand. He torqued a disk connected by nerves to his gut which was still reactive at times to the whole chore of digestion. This event precipitated a protracted downhill run with painkillers which he was able to manage until he wasn't. It was certainly the last of his tennis playing, but not the end of Lakewood. He still enjoyed going there with Margo, playing cards and having dinner, and being entertained by me with an occasional girlfriend demonstrating the latest dances of the mid-60s.

***

Meadowlark Lane was out by the Beltway, twelve miles from the center of DC, and a tough slog during heavy rush hour traffic to his job at Commerce. Paul didn't want to own two cars, and carpooling proved too difficult. But I had a car, a German-made VW in fact, which Paul gifted me despite some shit given him by relatives. I drove it with no compunction. While nominally attending George Washington University, I was still living at home (doing what?

Finding myself, perhaps). I'd drop off Paul on my way to classes at GW, quite close to the Federal Triangle. It was always tense, and it wouldn't take much to set one of us off, me in my way and he in his.

More often than not, though, Paul took the bus to work. He needed Margo to drive him to the bus stop, and from there it's an hour's ride, or an hour and a half if he missed the just-right rush hour window. Riding in, he'd read the NY Times and Washington Post, and a substantial book on the ride out. I have a clear image of him toting William Shirer's, *"Rise and Fall of the Third Reich,"* a best-seller at the time. Now of course, I wish he'd talked about it and everything related to it, but he never did (and I suppose I never asked).

Newsreel 1972-1992

1972–The Munich Olympics massacre, where eleven Israeli athletes were taken hostage and killed by the Palestinian group Black September. And Richard Nixon re-elected President of the US.

1973–The Paris Peace Accords are signed, leading to the end of U.S. involvement in the Vietnam War.

1974–President Nixon resigns following the Watergate scandal, and Gerald Ford becomes president.

1980–The U.S. Olympic hockey team defeats the Soviet Union in the "Miracle on Ice" at the Winter Olympics in Lake Placid.

1981–President Ronald Reagan takes office and begins implementing his economic policies, featuring significant cuts to income and capital gains tax, reducing government regulation, increased defense spending, and efforts to control inflation. This marks the beginning of a widening

income gap, reduced economic mobility, and the tripling of the national debt.

1985–The UN adopts Resolution 40/148 condemning Nazi, fascist, and neo-fascist activities and promoting democratic institutions. This resolution "condemns all totalitarian or other ideologies and practices, including Nazi, Fascist and neo-Fascist ideologies, based on racial or ethnic exclusiveness or intolerance, hatred and terror, which deprive people of basic human rights and fundamental freedoms and of equality of opportunity, and expresses its determination to combat those ideologies and practices.

1989–Fall of the Berlin Wall on November 9, marking the beginning of the end of the Cold War

1990–Reunification of Germany, officially ending the division between East and West Germany.

1991–The Strategic Arms Reduction Treaty (START I) is signed, leading to significant reductions in the nuclear arsenals of the United States and the Soviet Union. In 2021, the New START is signed.

1991–Dissolution of the Soviet Union on December 26, marking the end of the Cold War and the beginning of a new era in US-European relations.

1992–The Maastricht Treaty formally establishes the European Union (EU). It introduced "three pillars": Economic Community, Common Foreign and Security Policy, and Justice and Home Affairs, and made plans for a single currency (the Euro, introduced in 2002.) The aims of the European Union within its borders are: promote peace, its values and the well-being of its citizens. offer freedom, security and justice without internal borders. Every EU citizen enjoys the same fundamental rights based on the values of equality, non-discrimination, inclusion, human dignity, freedom and

democracy. These values are fortified and protected by the rule of law, spelled out in the EU Treaties and the Charter of Fundamental Rights.

Trips back in time

In the 1960s and 1970s Paul and Margo made occasional trips back to their old cities of Köln and Frankfurt. These always stirred strong feelings in them, with meaningful connections to their past, along with opportunities to update and recalibrate how far they'd come since. Sometimes these memories were raw, but always meaningful.

Paul went first, as early as 1950 and 1954, to gather information possibly useful for his pursuit of restitution. Margo came along in 1959. Köln had been almost totally destroyed and was largely unrecognizable. None of Paul's former homes or haunts existed. Margo's city of Frankfurt, on the other hand, was remarkably unscathed, the city being deemed of insufficient strategic value by both the Nazis and the Allies.

Later visits included Franklin and me. These visits—Paul, Margo, and us boys—usually involved driving along the Rhine, which is most beautiful between Frankfurt and Köln, their cities. We would have lunch along the way at a pleasant terrace in one of those small, picturesque towns like Bacharach or Assmannshausen. We boys remember the look on our parents' faces, a strange combination of bemused and sad, but overall, rather pleased with themselves. The old Jewish cemetery in Frankfurt was well-tended and completely undisturbed in the war. Generations of pre-war Kochs and Kahns lie peacefully under the large trees. One can spend hours there completely lost in time.

One such trip in the early 1970s included a special visit to Köln, where we were graciously hosted at the famous Dom Hotel by Anton and his wife Margaret and joined in a marvelous dinner by their son Heinrich and daughter Elizabeth. The next evening was another event with his old high school buddies, which went well into the night. It was a special reunion.

***

The Press Club organized interesting trips for its members, nominally to pursue background for journalistic stories and partly of course for pleasure. On one such trip Paul was able to take Margo along to the Baltic countries. Afterwards, Margo flew back to DC while Paul joined an organized side trip to Auschwitz.

Paul's visit to Auschwitz was one recollection of memories too far. Never one to talk about these memories, he was flung into a pit of despair and stayed there. Discussing feelings or memories was not something Paul ever did-ever. Instead, three predictable trends emerged: Paul took up alcohol and codeine with a vengeance ("to manage the pain" of the effects of war), I became a psychologist, social critic, and save-the-world type, and his younger son, by now showing signs of Aspergers and borderline personality disorder, dabbled in theater with a keen love of Shakespeare and drawing room comedy.

Another trip back went deep. It was in the early 1980s, well after Paul's visit to Auschwitz, with Paul and Margo. It featured first a gathering of surviving high school friends of Margo's from Frankfurt. None of them lived anymore in Frankfurt, of course, but a close friend living then in Lausanne organized a reunion in Lugano over a few days. Margo had a wonderful time with people she had not seen in years.

I joined them in Lugano and we then traveled by train to Frankfurt for a quick visit to the old Jewish cemetery, and the next day to Köln for another few days of organized activities re-uniting with Paul's Kölcher school buddies, this time without Anton who had passed a few years earlier.

On the last morning, Paul couldn't be roused. Not at all. He didn't seem dead but almost. None of us had seen him so comatose-like. He was like that for hours before he slowly came back to consciousness.

Frankly, I was surprised that he came back to life, and even a bit disappointed. Dying there would have been all right, I thought. Mother and I thought his collapse was most likely due to the stress of the situation—all that history culminating over a week's time in this moment in Köln, in the belly of the beast. But more recent speculation says Paul finally realized at least subconsciously after being with his old Kölcher buddies (none of whom was Jewish), that none had really stood up for him when the chips were down in the early 1930s—that he was essentially abandoned. One could say his friendship was betrayed.

In those dark hours after reminiscing around the table with his former friends, Paul surely came to recognize a terrible truth: he loved his Germany, but his Germany didn't love him back. With that recognition, slipping out of this life from his bed at Köln's comfortable Dom Hotel could be seen as a sensible, fitting end.

***

From the time Paul was carried off the US Military Hospital Ship Chateau-Thierry, he evolved in his role as a Restitution Warrior, wanting to restore the life justice demanded. He was successful, remarkably so, in getting financial compensation for losses incurred through theft by the Nazis and was acknowledged as one of the nation's leading restitution lawyers.

In this quest for justice and with his victories, he never *appeared* to feel victorious and never patted himself on the back for those victories. No gloats, no celebrations, no take that you fucking bastards. When he allowed himself the rewards of victory, to buy a new car, or a new home, or a new trip with his lovely Margo, or a college education for his two sons, he never spoke of the source of those gifts or what it meant to him to be such a provider.

Asked once while lying comfortably on his favorite *chaise longue* on his fine screen porch set in the oak woods of outer Bethesda, why he'd worked so hard to achieve all this, he said with startling clarity and some vehemence, "To prove that Hitler was wrong."

But he appeared saddest, and the most sanguine, when he realized that all that legal work, all those nights in his den pounding the typewriter, didn't really bring anything back, at least not those parts of life he most valued. Unfortunately, seeing the larger context of life in this world, the rebirth of bigotry in Europe and its variations in America, didn't help.

During all this time, Paul's health worsened. He made his visit to Auschwitz, which brought him low. He and I were estranged with some bitterness (due to the insult of insufficient recognition, apparently mutual) and I left home to pursue graduate studies in psychology, then settled in Minnesota to begin a career. My visits "home" were sorrowful ordeals, without any healing words or gestures. Paul declared his younger son Franklin a disappointment in words that cut deep. Margo, eager to calm the troubled waters but also despairing, consistently defended Frank. Paul, conflict averse, would retreat sullenly. These years were very tough on everyone.

Paul's stomach and lower back continued to give him problems, as did his self-medication with alcohol and codeine. A stint at a Minnesota chemical dependency treatment center helped a bit, but only a bit. When I picked him up after his requisite thirty days in residence, Paul insisted we go to the best steakhouse, preceded by, you guessed it, a martini. But treatment did have the effect of "ruining his drinking," an oft-stated consequence of treatment. Afterwards, in recognition of something, Paul made annual contributions to that clinic.

He continued to decline a few more years until he died, at home in his bed, in 1984. Moments before his last, he called out for Frank, napping somewhere at home in between unsuccessful forays in the so-called real world, and when he came, Paul asked where Mother was. Frank said she was outside tending the garden. Paul then said to him, using the language of farewell Paul and Margo first shared,

"Please tell her *á dieu*."

The next day, in a spasm of restored dignity, Margo hauled Paul's bed down from their shared bedroom and threw it out. She'd had enough. Some months earlier, I had suggested she consider leaving him. Paul, in his condition, had embarrassed her too often, I thought. She said she couldn't, "We've been through too much together." I understand.

***

Germany, to its credit, undertook many initiatives to come to terms with the horrors it had undertaken during the Third Reich.

It first submitted to a process of "denazification," a process initiated by the Allied forces to remove Nazi influence from public life, culture, press, economy, judiciary, and politics. It involved the removal of former Nazis from positions of power and influence.[37]

It invested heavily in education about the Holocaust and the Nazi era. This includes school curricula, public memorials, museums, and documentation centers dedicated to preserving the memory of the victims and educating future generations.[38]

Many German leaders have made numerous public apologies for the atrocities committed during the Nazi era. Commemorative events and ceremonies are held regularly to honor the victims and reflect on the past.[39]

For example, Frankfurt-am-Main conducted what they called a week-long "in-gathering of Jewish Exiles." These were done periodically over several years, and in 1991 the city of Frankfurt in-

---

[37] See "Why Germany Struggled to Reckon With the Nazi Past," https://jacobin.com/2023/07/germany-nazism-holocaust-federal-republic-memory-culture?form=MG0AV3

[38] See "After Hitler: Germany's Reckoning with the Nazi Past," https://www.hdg.de/en/haus-der-geschichte/exhibitions/after-hitler-germanys-reckoning-with-the-nazi-past

[39] Jacobin.com op cit

vited my mother and her two brothers, along with probably hundreds of others they could still locate, with costs paid by the City. I came along. In a large assembly they were greeted by the Mayor who spoke from the heart, and invited everyone to dinner. There were panel discussions and visits to important sites. My mother and uncles were invited to speak at their former schools, where they answered dozens of penetrating questions from young adolescents eager to learn from the ultimate authorities on those times. "Why didn't you leave earlier? Why didn't you fight back?" Variations of those questions were the ones most frequently asked, and I watched my elders struggle to answer. It was never easy.

These initiatives reflect Germany's ongoing commitment to acknowledging and learning from its history to ensure that such atrocities are never repeated. But these programs were conducted only in West Germany. Cities in East Germany, long a satellite of the Soviet Union before the two Germanys were re-united, never created the opportunity to come to terms with its Nazi past. It's probably no coincidence that this is where today's most right-wing political party is rising to new power.

***

Fortunately, and Paul would certainly agree with this sentiment, Margo transitioned well into the next chapter of her life. Over the next ten years, she continued her work with The Agency and was able to broaden her social activities, often with her friend Clarence Siegal. Clarence, a colleague from Paul's earliest days at Commerce, and his wife Jeannie were best friends with Paul and Margo from the beginning. Two of the brightest people I ever met, they were both second generation Americans with advanced degrees in international commerce and labor statistics, and together they'd gone to Washington in the early FDR years to be of help in building out The New Deal.

The four of them frequently played bridge together, went to dinner together, and travelled together to Jamaica on vacation. When Jeannie and Paul passed away within a few months of each other, Clarence and Margo became "frequent guests" at each other's home. Both Frank and I were completely surprised but totally delighted at this development, as Clarence was consistently good to Margo and had been in many ways the American father we boys never had. We both loved him.

When Margo realized the house on Meadowlark was too big, especially after Frank moved to Minneapolis to live closer to me, she moved into the nearby "Classic Residence by Hyatt," a senior living facility that thankfully was run by the hotel industry rather than the medical establishment. She thrived during her ten years there, leading the German club, the French club, the Radio Theater club, and gently facilitating the organ recitals (her term) that broke out at the Hyatt breakfast tables ("my legs… my eyes… my heart…"). She then ascended to the presidency of the Residents' Council.

Margo travelled back to Germany a number of times with her brother Eric in a ritual they called "ancestor worship," tracking down interesting points of family history. One was that Dr. Hermann Koch of Geisa, the progenitor of the Koch line and father of the jeweler Robert Koch, was the direct descendant of Napoleon, having been conceived in a fit of celebration after the battle of Jena. Every generation of Kochs, including me, was brought up to believe this story. Everything about it seemed right, or at least convenient. Unfortunately, Eric and Margo found the proper gravestone, suggesting that Hermann's mother would have to have been pregnant almost thirty months for the story to be true. *C'est dommage.* I've had to retract all my cocktail party claims of descent from "our liberator." Other trips pursued newly discovered near-relations caught up in bizarre fashion in the rabid Nazi events of the '30s, patrons of the Koch store, and other characters who became subjects of Eric's interesting histories.⁴⁰

Margo provided an interview in 1996 to the University of Southern California Shoah Foundation, founded by Steven Spielberg, in which she describes her life growing up in liberal, assimilated Frankfurt in the Weimar years, her slow but steady preparation for emigration as its necessity grew from 1932 to 1938, life with Paul as they fled Germany for England amidst growing threats and fears, and her gratitude for their life in America. Most of the sentiments she expressed in this interview found their way into this book.⁴¹

Margo had a good life at the Hyatt, with additional travels and visits with Frank, Jean (my first wife), me, Susan, and all her other Koch and Kahn relatives, and was without ailment or complaint until she suffered a massive and completely unexpected stroke while toasting the arrival of the New Year going into 2004, at the age of ninety-one. She enjoyed two memorial services, one for family and one for her Washington friends, and against convention was survived by her two *younger* brothers, who both lived until their late 90s.

Margo Koch Mayer, 2002

---

40   Eric's biography and links to his extensive work are at https://en.wikipedia.org/wiki/Eric_Koch. His YouTube channel, in which he provides interesting stories of the Koch and Kahn family is at https://www.youtube.com/eokoch

41   Interview of Margaret Mayer, July 31, 1996, in the archive of the University Southern California Shoah Foundation Institute for Visual History and Education. Interviewee code 17552. For more information: https://sfi.usc.edu

Steven's Tale: *"Mein Kampf, Part II"*

Time for a little personal storytelling that relates to my father and the Nazis.

Two years into my hitch as an entry-level professor at a semi-major university in its Psychology Department "The University of Georgia? What's wrong with Harvard? Is that the best you can do?" Paul asked me. Attempting to resemble a professor, I realized I had nothing to profess. I didn't really want to serve the field of psychology, the university, or academia in general. I wanted to do something more useful.

I moved back to Minneapolis and earnestly hung out my shingle in a two-room Humphrey Bogart-like office, doing business as "Rainbow Research," a name inspired over breakfast at the Rainbow Café, the name chosen for my practice to set myself apart from "Control Data, Inc.," a now defunct but then Fortune 500 crosstown rival, sort of.

It didn't take long before I recognized the shadow of my father hanging over me as I hunched over my typewriter (this was pre-Radio Shack Model 1), working on my nonprofit program evaluation projects, critiquing community development and social justice programs and the foundations that support them. I asked myself, "Why am I doing this work? And for whom? And is it really mine or an extension of a whole lot of stuff that happened or didn't happen between my father and me?" A few bouts with psychological counseling allowed me to claim the vocational part as mine, while recognizing that "being an evaluator" is a mental tendency in pursuit of fair and reasonable judgments that I probably received from my father.

After his death, the anger I had felt towards my father slowly began to dissolve, and in 1994 as I turned fifty I took a sabbatical from Rainbow Research and spent three months in Paris. I found myself toting my father around on my shoulder as he'd whisper into my ear, "How about we go to Roland Garros today for the French

Open tennis semis?" or "Let's have a cognac at the Hotel Intercontinental and celebrate the Liberation of Paris!" or "Let's take another look at my old apartment building across from St. Julien le Pauvre, where your beautiful mother would come to visit me in the afternoon." I often see Paris through their eyes.

During that sabbatical I had occasion to go to the Czech Republic and visit Theresienstadt, the concentration camp where Paul's parents were sent in 1943. On my return to Paris, I wrote an article and sent it to the New Yorker magazine, which almost accepted it (judging by the amount of time they took to reject it.) It's called *"Mein Kampf,* Part II." The original *Mein Kampf* is, of course, the book Adolph Hitler wrote in prison while still an out-of-power rabble rouser, describing his dreams for the German people. But the title is simply translated into English as "My Struggle," and it's in this sense that I chose the title. Written in 1994, it introduces many of the themes of this book, but brings out the relationship among me, my father, and his father.

"Mein Kampf, Part II" (1994)

"Oh, you mean Therezin?" the information counterman in Prague's railroad station asked me. "The concentration camp? What the Germans called Theresienstadt?" I startled at his abrupt and pointed reply. But indeed, that is what I meant. "Go to the bus terminal and take number 29. It goes right there. Takes an hour."

I'd been living in Paris for a few months and had the opportunity to visit Prague as part of a quick tour of the East. I was studying a map of the Czech Republic and spotted Therezin, not really looking for it. I telephoned my mother, living in Washington DC. "Have you been there?" I asked. "Had Dad?" I knew my father had visited Auschwitz, where both his parents were killed. But no, she said, neither had been to Theresienstadt, where my grandparents had spent more than two whole years before being shipped to Auschwitz and fed to the ovens. I decided to go.

On the bus to Therezin, I reviewed what I knew of my grandparents. It wasn't much. My father barely ever spoke of them. Not because of disaffection or alienation—far from it. But my father's wounds from that period had never healed, and he wasn't given to talk about painful subjects. The one time I ever saw him cry was when I, as a teenager, asked him about his parents. He began to oblige me, but soon dissolved into uncontrollable sobs. End of conversation. I knew little.

I knew my grandfather Ernst was a physician, born in Trier in the Mosel valley, who moved as a young man to begin a medical practice in the old German city of Köln (Cologne, in the French spelling). He was said to be a stern man but capable, on occasion, of spoiling his son. After the Nazis had established themselves in power, he and his wife Elizabeth, whose family was from Metz in Lorraine, were rounded up by the Gestapo in June 1942 and "sent East" to Theresienstadt.

Theresienstadt was where Jews too prominent to kill just yet were taken. There, my grandfather was made to be a camp doctor, my grandmother to teach needlework to the other wives and daughters. The Nazis made Theresienstadt a "showplace." They made propaganda movies of it and gave tours to officials of the World Council of Churches, the International Red Cross, and the U.S. Department of State, to demonstrate how kindly the German Third Reich was treating its Jews. The movie shows residents of the town playing bridge and doing embroidery on a hotel terrace and attending chamber music recitals.

But towards the end of 1944, with the approach from the East of the Red Army and the growing recognition that the days of the "Thousand Year Reich" were numbered, the Nazi leadership decided to expedite their work on the "final solution to the Jewish problem." On October 28, my grandparents were sent together to Auschwitz, on train number 1073, as noted in the books by the ever-efficient Germans, where they disappeared in ashes and smoke.

My parents had escaped that fate, though barely. They met each other for the first time in 1933 in Paris, in line for service at the offices of the *Agence Internationale des Droits de l'Homme*, where they were seeking information on how their German visas would be affected by the newest regulations announced by the Nazis, who had come to power just months earlier. Already there were new laws prohibiting Jews from entering the professions, and my father's career as an attorney, just seven days old after being admitted to the bar, came to an abrupt and arbitrary end. He frequently spoke of how he could return his newly purchased attorney's robe to the store, unused. He had gone to Paris to explore what options he might have there when a new set of decrees further limiting the rights of Germany's Jewish citizens came out.

My mother had been sent to Paris as a nineteen-year-old from her family home in Frankfurt, for the customary (for young women in families of her standing) year at the Sorbonne. Her grandfather had begun a jewelry store in Frankfurt that flourished in the new wealth that flooded Germany after it had defeated the French in 1870. It rose to prominence and sold its *de luxe* custom jewelry to the crowned heads of Europe until the Great War, becoming "the Tiffany's" of Germany. The store continued its success in family hands until the advent of the Nazis, when it was forcibly sold to "Aryan interests," though it kept the family name (Koch) even until its closing in 1989.

But in 1933 my mother was living in a *"pension en famille"* near the Jardin du Luxembourg, a *pension* that still exists and where I am now sitting writing this very story.

My parents met and romanced in Paris. But no good career options emerged for my father, and he returned to Köln. My mother later joined him there, and they married in 1936. While prescient, fearful, or adventurous Jews were leaving Germany in large numbers, my father could not bring himself to believe that the official and deliberate anti-Semitic policies of the regime were meant for him. Besides, he was a German first, and passionately loved Germany. His father was a decorated field physician in the Kaiser's army. His identity as a Jew was slight, almost incidental, even though his great-grandfather had been a rabbi, and he had been *bar mitzvah*'ed. He believed, as did all too many German Jews, that this thing with the Nazis would blow over.

It was only after Kristallnacht on November 8-9, 1938, that he recognized the threat. On that night, hooligans sacked and destroyed synagogues and looted Jewish-owned stores throughout Germany, all under the approving eyes of the sponsoring Gestapo, the Nazi state police. My parents, to be safe, had earlier prepared distant relatives living in the States to vouch for and sponsor their immigration should trouble come. The U.S. State Department was operating a strict quota system, allowing in only a few Jews each year. My parents used the sponsorship of their relatives in Louisiana to gain admission to England, where they had to wait a year before gaining permission to enter the U.S in January 1940.

By then the war had started in Europe, the Germans invading and occupying lands first to its east, then to its west and north, without even a declaration of war. My parents were living in New York, barely eking out a living, when the U.S., officially neutral in the events in Europe, was finally pulled into the war after the events at Pearl Harbor in December 1941. My father enlisted, at the age of thirty-five, and he reported eagerly. It took quite a while for the U.S. Army to figure out what to do with him, but they finally recognized that his knowledge of German and Germany might be useful. They finally sent him to the Military Intelligence Training Center at Camp Ritchie to become one of the famed "Ritchie Boys," and sent him to France soon after D-Day as part of a unit that interrogated captured German forces.

By the fall of 1944, eleven years after meeting my mother in Paris, my father found himself there again, now in the uniform of the U.S. Army. I had just been born in New York, and Paris had just been liberated from four years of German occupation. My father eagerly awaited the Allied advance east across the Rhine, to rescue his parents. He knew by then his parents had been sent to Theresienstadt, but he did not know that at that very moment they were about to be sent to Auschwitz.

Before heading for Therezin I spent three days absorbing beautiful old Prague, which according to my tour guide is "the oldest city that has never been destroyed." Prague had once been home to a thriving Jewish community and is now host to the oldest active synagogue in all of Europe. When all of Europe was in Hitler's thrall, Jewish communities were decimated. But Hitler decided to save Prague's Jewish quarter, to keep it intact as a museum, a museum "to an extinct race," he hoped, and he worked with fervor and dedication to make it so. Of Czechoslovakia's 300,000 Jews before the war, fewer than 3,000 remain. But unique in all of Europe, the Jewish community's old buildings are still intact in Prague's old Jewish quarter.

My bus pulled into the town of Therezin, after traveling through pleasant Bohemian countryside. But I became confused. The bus had just passed what was clearly an old prison camp, and billboards announced a museum there. A discreet Star of David suggested this was indeed the place. But I thought my grandparents were kept in the town, and there was a museum there as well. My grandmother's mother had also been sent to Therezin and had died "naturally," it was said, having collapsed "in her kitchen;" that suggested town living. Perhaps, I thought, they lived in the town, and my grandfather worked in the prison camp.

I chose to go to the camp first, walking the quarter mile out of town. I mustered my courage, telling myself Therezin was only a concentration camp, not a "death camp." It shouldn't be as bad, I told myself, as an Auschwitz or a Buchenwald.

Slipping by the admission window (who pays to get *inside* a concentration camp?), I briefly tagged along with a tour group whose guide told us this particular prison had been filled with a mix of people: Jews and Gypsies, most of whom were sent on to death camps. But at least half, she said, were political prisoners, largely Czech resistors to the Nazi regime. These were sometimes given a trial and then shot, some were sent home, and others sent to worse places. The years 1943 and 1944 were particularly hard, she said, irrespective of origins, epidemics of one kind or another swept through the camp, killing most.

Leaving the group and turning a corner, I was suddenly alone and came face to face with what the brochure called "the doctor's office." Not at all expecting this, and quite shocked, I decided this must be my very own grandfather's office!

There, behind a set of prison bars placed firmly in the doorway, was a room "restored" to suggest a doctor's office, with three gray desks and tables with strange testing devices placed on them. In one corner, set at an angle in an almost aesthetic gesture, was a medical supplies cabinet, full of small bottles behind a glass front.

An image of my grandfather floated in front of me, first as I remembered him in the photograph that had hung above my father's bed. But then he became animated, and moved about the room, thoughtfully but gracefully, a now-solid figure in a grey suit. He took some bottles out of the cabinet and set them about on the tables, while he put other things back into the cabinet. He was alone, but just off to the side one could see, even enter, one of those rooms with the kind of endless bunk beds one sees in the newsreels, beds crammed with emaciated bodies too sick and desperate to move—his waiting room.

But who was waiting for what, I wondered? What purpose does a doctor serve in a concentration camp? Was his job to keep people fit enough to be sent to the ovens? Why bother? I was filled with dark thoughts about the Nazi purpose.

I peered into his office. He seemed not to be distressed with the surroundings, but was intent on doctorly things, keeping up "his" office like the good professional I'm sure he was. When the Gestapo had first knocked on the door of his Köln office, he said he couldn't go with them, that he had surgery scheduled in just a few hours. And he told his son and daughter-in-law, in the hours after Kristallnacht, that they should flee but that he could not leave Germany, that all his patients were depending on him.

I began to talk to him, first about his son Paul, my father. I told him how his son loved him and had tried desperately to find him. "But you know all that," I found myself saying, but even so, I needed more to continue this presentation to my grandfather. I told him how his son had gotten as far as Paris, a sergeant in the U.S. Army following the advancing Allies from the beaches of Normandy. I told him how my father lived for the day the Allies could push across the Rhine and destroy the fucking Nazi war machine and the madmen at its controls so he could find and free his parents and restore his own life. But my father was never to make it. Consumed with worry, he collapsed in Paris with bleeding ulcers. He was rushed to the American Hospital in Neuilly, and barely survived emergency surgery. In December 1944 he was shipped back to England and then further back to upstate New York where he had to finish out the war in an Army hospital. A few months after the war ended in Europe, and three years after they were abducted from their home in Köln, he learned of his parents' fate.

My father spent the rest of his life in mourning. He never found any real peace in his new country. Where others were able to piece together a new and meaningful life, with children, new careers, new friends and interests, my father was not. He lived an uprooted and alienated life until he died, an event surely hastened by a visit be made to Auschwitz in 1979, where he suffered a breakdown of sorts from which he never recovered. He pulled the plug on himself, dying three years later, weighing eighty-five pounds, from what could have been called a lack of appetite. "He looks," said an innocent nurse's aide at the end, "like someone from one of those concentration camp movies."

I was ready to leave and walked away. But aware of feeling not yet finished, I came back. I wanted to slip through the bars that separated me from my grandfather in his "restored doctor's office" and sit across the table from him so I could tell him of myself, his older grandson, born in New York as he inhabited this very office.

I told him how so much of my life has been marked and shaped by this history, this story of uncompleted exodus in which some succeeded in their flight from fascism, others were caught and destroyed, and others, even survivors and their offspring, held in a kind of amber until something frees them. I told him of my own work, my struggles, my loves, and my fears, and how they all had strong, clear connection to his life in this little prison cell.

And I told him of my anger, never far from the surface. These months in Paris I'd been reliving and claiming much of the past. I saw the city lovingly, through my parents' eyes of sixty years earlier. The city's newspapers were reprinting daily their lead stories from fifty years earlier, the days between D-Day and Liberation Day, and I wept as I suddenly recognized how unthinkably criminal it was that a city as beautiful and joyful as Paris should come under the iron heel of the fucking fascist Germans.

On D-Day I went to the Intercontinental Hotel by the Place Vendôme, where the German High Command had been garrisoned, and in the bar over martinis (my father's drink) toasted the destruction of the German nation. On Liberation Day I stood in front of the German Embassy and shouted *"Vive la France! Vive les Juifs! Morts aux Boches!"* And whenever I read about skinheads and their neo-fascism in "modern Germany," I draft a letter to the International Herald Tribune calling for "a final solution to the German problem."

My grandfather was unmoved. I stood there, beginning to feel uncomfortable, shifting from one foot to another, not knowing what to do. Occasionally tourists would come through. I had the urge to talk. I picked out one family, and because they were speaking Dutch

I took a chance on them. Engaging them in English, I startled them. "This is my grandfather's office," I said. They reacted well, and pretended I was not a lunatic. They listened and asked sensitive questions. "This must be a very emotional moment for you," the mother said. I nodded dumbly, barely aware of the drama I must be creating for them.

They left, and I turned to talk to my grandfather again. "Were you here," I wondered, "when the Nazis made their propaganda movies?" He probably was. He must have hoped desperately they hadn't fooled anyone. Surely officials of the World Council of Churches, the International Red Cross, and the U.S. Department of State, for whom the films were primarily made, would not believe the Nazis sent these people East to play cards, make music, and do embroidery for the next thousand years. Regrettably, these officials did not question what they were shown, and the top leaders of the world's churches, charities, and democracies never raised a peep against the genocide that was taking place in over a dozen factories of human extermination throughout the area.

Did he even know about Auschwitz and the other camps? It's quite possible, even likely. Rumors must have swept through the camp with every load of new arrivals. By the time my grandparents were themselves being pushed into those infamous cattle cars bound for Auschwitz, they must certainly have known what awaited them.

How could he work with such knowledge, not just the knowledge of his own fate, but that of all the others? He looked up at me. "How can I *not* work like this, even with such knowledge? There have always been genocides, and they continue even in your world in your time," he said. "We mortals seem to have learned only doctoring; we don't know how to *prevent* the pathology of fascism, or how to keep those with genocidal instincts from power. All doctors' waiting rooms look like mine."

I tried again to leave. This time I got as far as the gift shop, where I bought a Star of David to wear around my neck, the first I'd ever worn. I came back to my grandfather's office and said a Kaddish, the Jewish prayer for the dead, spiritually joining my grandfather with the ages, with eternal truths and beliefs.

Then, an impulse grew in me. I had brought with me to Paris a bracelet belonging to my father, an identity bracelet from his Army days, engraved with "Sgt Paul Mayer, ID# 32428055." It was not "general issue" Army wear, but a piece of jewelry he apparently bought in Paris in that autumn of 1944. I'd never seen him wear it, but I took possession of it when he died, and I wore it occasionally on his birthday and other times of commemoration. I'd worn it to the Intercontinental on D-Day, to ponder the unbelievable set of circumstances that allowed me to be sitting there.

And I wore it to Therezin. Standing there in front of my grandfather's office I took it off, and carefully taking aim, tossed it through the bars so that it skittered along the floor and through a small opening directly underneath my grandfather's medical supplies cabinet! It will never be seen and will be there another fifty years at least. My father and grandfather were finally reunited, and I with them.

I was finally done. I could leave, and began to, but was distracted by something happening in my grandfather's office. From outside, through a small prison window I'd barely noticed had flown a small, white butterfly. It fluttered around my grandfather's office a few times and then flitted behind his medical supplies cabinet. Just moments later, *two* butterflies emerged from that spot. They flew once more around the room, and then, after seeming to pause briefly in front of me, flew out the window together.

Wrapping up

The truth about Paul

Truth to tell, I never actually heard my father speak against the Nazis. Never heard "fucking Nazis" or anything like that. Of course, there was much he never said. Maybe he couldn't bring himself to utter their name.

Paul's hurts were unspoken, except by me. I've spoken of them all my life. Paul's hurts became my hurts, as displayed fully in "*Mein Kampf,* Part II." Paul hankered for his old Germany even after the war and would have moved back there if Margo were agreeable, he said, but she wasn't.

As I began this writing project, I connected with Anton's son from Köln, Heinrich, my age, who had occasion as an adult to visit Washington where he had business. He sang Paul's praises to me, "Paul had a strong sense of honor, a skilled analysis of current events, and a way of rejecting false authority-an interesting character," he said in salute.

Paul was a stalwart persistent character, a quiet and principled warrior, a warrior with a typewriter in a fight for understanding and fairness—call it justice—a fight that he pursued with every skill that he had, a fight born of a grievance but moderated by understanding, understanding of the German character and devotion to justice as we imagine is articulated in his great grandfather's three-volume book on the subject of Rights.[42] He would make his case, take the high road, and resort to principled arguments with skillful parries and thrusts. They don't give awards for his kind of service.

In this story, Paul had to counter the force of the mighty Nazis from 1930 on. He was able to do this successfully only after the war, in legal demands for restitution, a right afforded him through the merciful actions of the victors. He couldn't be the corporate lawyer he was trained to be and expected to be and would have been if the Nazis hadn't come to power and taken all his rights and standing away. Instead, he became an advocacy lawyer like his great-great-grandfather Samuel pleading his case to the powers that be in Hechingen, most notably the Hohenzollern prince, the epitome of almost two thousand years of Germanism.

Paul was a rule of law guy rooted in the study of law, political science, and economics. He lived in a Germany that was steeped in regard for the law and simultaneously, disregard for the law. His own tradition of law, inherited from his forefathers, ran deep and clear. By the time he entered formal law training, the nation's law was finally enshrined in a Constitution. Until it wasn't, shredded by powerful angry grievance-ridden forces that simply tore it up and proclaimed their fucking selves to be superior to anyone and everyone who disagreed with them. Rule of law? My law, the new sheriff said, under penalty of deprivation, deportation, and death. And he had the people with him. There is still disbelief in how he pulled that off, even as people at this time hear the echoes of that time.

There are always powerful forces that oppose the rule of law, somewhere below the surface and sometimes at the surface. They arise and they subside, often without explanation or understanding, but that rhythm has marked recorded history since history was

---

42 I hope to find someday a readable version of his book, which is probably tucked away in some dusty German archive. It was surely printed in an old Gothic German font, impenetrable even by Google.

first recorded. Those forces, known as autocracy, authoritarianism, or tyranny want to disrupt the rule of law that serves the greater good and replace it with their own autocratic dictatorial rules born from ignorance, greed, whimsy, grievance, and malice. Paul, in his reasoned and soft-spoken way, stood against the corruption such ill-conceived power represents.

When asked why he'd worked so hard for so long to gain a measure of justice by reclaiming some portion of what was stolen, he said clearly and forcefully, "to prove Hitler was wrong." Pretty amazing, if you ask me. What's not said in that statement is anything like vengeance, or even self-righteousness.

And how is this proof that Hitler was wrong to be offered? And through what lens of law does he pursue his vision of justice? American law? Weimar law? Enlightenment law? The human rights law of the Hebrews, Greeks, or Romans that his great-grandfather Samuel reveled in? Post-war Universal Declaration of Human Rights law? Yes, yes, yes to all.

That's what I imagine occupied Paul's fevered brain, wounded heart, and aggrieved soul as he bent over his righteous typewriter, offering up "the proof that Hitler was wrong."

My epiphany

Did Paul ever find peace within himself? Not really. Not at all, actually. It certainly hurt that he was forced from his homeland, that he lost his parents to the unspeakable (there's a clue) brutality of the Nazis, that he lived in exile most of his adult life.

Did he succeed in overcoming the 1933, 1938, and 1944 versions of the fucking Nazis? Well, no. He didn't overcome but he was quietly defiant and persistent. All those times that I've portrayed him here as indecisive, whether to stay or to go? A different interpretation is that he was *completely* decisive. He decided to stay, and he was insistent. "No one can tell me I don't belong here!" That's a very clear and deep statement of belief.

When you think about the litany of injustices he suffered, the brutality of the force that wanted to disregard him a rightful human being and make him disappear, and the equally forceful presentations of his rights that would later prove in a court of law that Hitler was wrong, it's easier to see his courage and determination. And, one could say, his heroism. For that, I love him. He deserves a medal and everyone's full respect, and certainly mine.

It's at this point in my own writing, wishing to understand my father and what drove him, that I had an epiphany. Throughout this project, the working title of my book was "My Father Against the Fucking Nazis." But now, recognizing that the anger expressed in that phrasing was mine and not Paul's, I allowed myself to drop "fucking" from the title.

That's not to say I think of those Nazis with equanimity. No, no, no! In my thoughts, I still can't say Nazis without saying fucking Nazis. When I watch today's Newsreels I see plenty of aspiring Nazis. When I tell people I'm writing a book called "My Father Against the Fucking Nazis," I'm applauded. But that's me talking, not Paul. Watching today's news lets us see the same growing forces of nationalized ignorance and greed trying to have their own lawless way with others; those forces are clearly on the rise again.

So I haven't dropped my anger entirely – I just don't want to give the power of recognition to the current crop of fucking Nazis. One can still hope, and I do, as my neighbor Anne Frank proposed, that the good that is in peoples' hearts at birth is not finally extinguished and forced into submission, but is allowed and encouraged to rise up and smite the forces of evil injustice we all-too-often feel getting ever-closer.

I can feel hope, but I'm not optimistic. Even though we Americans are blessed with a system of law and justice based on inalienable rights and honed over the years with a judicial system that while not at all perfect still bends in the direction of improving the lives lived in this noble experiment called democracy, it's at grave risk of collapsing through the intentionally destructive actions of the rising tyranny of unlawful and corrupt behavior ascending to the highest places of our government.

***

I think my father would allow this final act of theater, staged from my imagination, perhaps a musical:

Me: "Where have all the Nazis gone? Did they drop off the face of the earth when they allegedly surrendered in 1945 and go to some afterlife place where they're sentenced to eternity? No, they didn't disappear, they just went underground until the time is right to reappear. They went all over the world, joining kindred spirits."

Grandfather Ernst: "I'm afraid much of our current situation can be explained by the legacy of our old princes, kings, and emperors, even the Holy Roman Emperors that were neither Holy nor Roman, that ruled much of Europe and beyond for centuries. They hated Jews and Muslims, and destroyed, raped and pillaged our communities whenever they had the chance. They financed their so-called Holy Crusades with the spoils. The map of much of the world today is easily traced to their war-faring ways."

Great grandfather Adolf: "I spent several years in America. Too many Germans, IMO. On the boat over was a man named Trumpf–anyone seen him? I can imagine his type is popular with all those kindred spirits Steven speaks of."

Brother Frank: "To be or not to be, that is the question."

Great-great-grandfather Rabbi Samuel Mayer, perhaps the real hero of this story: It's hard to stay hopeful, to carry hope to others so that ultimately all are treated fairly and with respect. That's what we must hope for, work for, and live for."

Their wives Margo, Lisbeth, Frederiecke, Sara, with the last word: "Men! Jeez…"

A visit to the Hechingen Synagogue

It's time to go back to the beginning of this book, and visit Hechingen and its Synagogue, once presided over by my great-great-grandfather Rabbi Samuel Mayer.

To get there, we rented a car in Frankfurt, and first drove through the Rhineland, searching out old Mayer, Teutsch, Kahn and Koch town sites and their cemeteries.

Old Jewish cemeteries are memorable oases of permanence and permanent oases of memory. The solid, weathered headstones whisper, "We're here! We're still here! Thank you for visiting and remembering!" The ashes of those victims of genocidal fascism that were shot skyward have settled here to visit as well. The feelings these forlorn but well-maintained cemeteries evoke—how to possibly describe those? It's all the bittersweet taste of memory, of what we know and what we now realize we don't know about the person right here laid to rest at our feet, memorialized with stone. One wonders about the qualities of that person. "Just how are we related? What do we share?" And the shade of the very old trees gathered in protective shelter for all time, alive with the chatter of wise birds also come to visit.

Hechingen Synagogue, March 2022

And finally, we came to the Jewish cemetery of Hechingen. We found the stone that marks Samuel's resting place, reposed in the past.

Here's a photo of Samuel's grave, and an English translation of the inscription.

Rabbi Samuel Mayer gravestone, Hechingen Cemetery, March 2022

Dr. Samuel Mayer
Rabbi of the local community
and Lawyer
born 5 January 1807
died 1 August 1875
A faithful husband
A good father
A noble man
A dutiful official
A great scholar
Who has done enough for
The best of his time
has lived for all time

When my father died, he was given a memorial service at our home on Meadowlark, convened by Margo and attended by Illa, all his in-laws, and me and my brother, with a genuine rabbi hired to recite the necessary prayers. Sitting comfortably in our living room, everyone spoke heartfelt and meaningful tributes to Paul.

But he never had a gravestone. He had given his body over for study by the medical students of George Washington University. His remains were cremated *per* his own instructions, and no one thought to ask for his ashes.

So, I hereby offer up a gravestone, engraved using Paul's own great-grandfather Samuel's gravestone as a template, adding in italics a bit of tribute of my own.

> He was a faithful husband.
> *He always adored his Margarete, respected her, and wanted nothing more than to show her a good time.*
>
> He was a good father.
> *Well, his intentions were good, and somehow he managed to instruct both his children to act honorably.*
>
> He was a noble man.
> *He carried himself with dignity, without fail.*
>
> He was a dutiful official.
> *He brought upstanding values to everything he worked on.*
>
> He was a great scholar.
> *Maybe not great but good enough (poetic engraver's license). Actually, he was marvelously insightful and insisted on finding good answers to decent questions. The identity of "Cassandrus" also fits.*
>
> Who has done enough for the best of his time that has lived for all time.
> *He brought good stuff into this world, contributing far more of value than he took.*

Re-dedication of my book

I'm now back on my Amsterdam rooftop, with another cigar from Hajenius, musing. Thankfully the Allies won the war, the city was not destroyed, and the view of this 750 year old city is much the same as it was eighty years ago. The bells of the West Church were melted down by the fucking Nazis to make artillery, but they were replaced soon after they fled in May 1945, and they again ring every quarter hour. Trains still leave towards Germany every quarter hour, and while I'm surprised that Germans are permitted in this city, trains arrive from there just as often.

...and musing about Paul. Understanding him and his story–our story–has been quite an undertaking, the work of a lifetime. It's been kind of an obsession, I have to admit. I'd noticed earlier that my relationship with him began to improve when he died forty years ago. And writing it now in such depth marks a kind of a passage from obsession to completion, I surely hope.

Through this writing process, I've pondered my father and his journey from childhood through the twists and turns of his obstacle-strewn life. I've come to understand and appreciate him ever so much more. I'm now moved to create a new dedication of this book, to take its place as a second stanza to the one to offered to my mother at its beginning. I could have put it there, but here at the end seems fitting, given all we've been through.

>Dedicated to my father
>Paul A. Mayer
>
>With new-found Affection,
>Appreciation,
>
>Thanks,
>and a kiss on the cheek.
>
>*Ich liebe dich!*

Paul A. Mayer, 1969, age 62, looking good

Acknowledgements

I would like to acknowledge and thank a few contributors to my telling of this story.

First, there's the persistent motive power of memory, both mine and others'. Stories of righteous resistance to unholy brutality have lit up our imaginations for millennia. Long live the storytellers!

Second, there's my uncle Eric Koch, who was also stung at an early age by the song of memory and coached me to an appreciation of history and our family's place in it.

There are a few people from my childhood who remember Paul and have miraculously stayed in touch with me and encouraged me to write. Paul Knutson and Jane Lake get special mention.

Along the way I was helped by two gifted psychotherapists, Joan Churchill and Charlotte Ketcham; both helped me to finally distinguish myself from my father. Robert Beatty, Dharma teacher, helped me discover my own right way forward. And Jelle van Andel, Tao acupuncturist, kept me grounded and vital.

There's two people who coaxed this written story out of me, Ian Graham Leask of Calumet Editions and Afton Press, and Lajos Egri, author of *The Art of Dramatic Writing*. And thanks to Gary Lindberg, Josh Weber and Blake Cipperly for their hard work at Calumet Editions.

Recently re-entering my life is Heinrich Comes, the son of my father's best friend from the before times, who stepped forward to embrace me just as his father had embraced mine.

Gratitude to the people of Mokum who provided safe harbor these last many years, especially Jaap de Graaf and Ruth Dreier, and of course to Anne Frank, who got me started.

And thanks to those Americans who actually do make America great; may they prevail.

Special thanks go to my many circles and sub-circles of friends in Minneapolis, past and present, who in their own way have encouraged me to tell my story. I feel a special kinship with all these soul sisters and brothers and am grateful for you in my life.

Finally, I can't possibly say or give enough thanks to my own very special source of encouragement and companionship, my ever-loving partner, girlfriend, travel companion, and co-discoverer - Susan Doherty! Thanks, babe…

About the Author

The author, wearing his father's escape coat.

Steven E. Mayer is the son of this story's protagonist. He became a consulting psychologist and founded the nonprofit Rainbow Research, Inc, dedicated to helping socially concerned organizations respond more effectively to social problems and opportunities. His professional insights are shared in his book, *How to Save the World: Evaluating Your Choices*, and on his website, EffectiveCommunities.com. With hindsight one can see that his work was informed by his experience growing up with his father.

-Amsterdam, 2025

www.ingramcontent.com/pod-product-compliance
Lightning Source LLC
Chambersburg PA
CBHW020230170426
43201CB00007B/374